C000245005

ABOUT THE AUTH

Doug Tucker left his inner-London comprehensive school at sixteen and a half with no real academic qualifications and soon followed his dream of joining the Royal Marine Commandos, where he served a successful military career. He then followed in the footsteps of many ex-servicemen and sought employment in public services, in his case becoming a full-time firefighter for eight years. Wanting more of a challenge and to improve his lot in life, Doug set out on a series of ventures, some successful and others less so, ultimately resigning from the fire service to run his own company importing garden leisure equipment from America and Africa. His company grew to become one of the largest dealers in luxury garden spas in the world, winning awards for sales and marketing achievements. Over time, Doug progressed into the financial services industry, where he enjoyed great success working for a world-leading organisation, travelling the world and mentoring financial services sales professionals. The experience led him to build his own company, Sales Commando, where he has packaged the lessons he has learnt throughout his life. His aim is to provide breakthrough moments for people who want to develop and get to the next level in sales.

Today, Doug Tucker holds motivational and educational seminars around the world and has improved the sales techniques of thousands who have attended these events.

Transform your sales career today.

www.sales-commando.com

Financial Services

SALES COMMANDO

UNLEASH YOUR POTENTIAL

Doug Tucker

PG Press – PGP

Published by PG Press (PGP)

Mountain Farmhouse, Marden Road,
Marden, Kent TN12 9PZ
Telephone: +44 (0) 1622 831310
info@pgpress.co.uk
www.pgpress.co.uk

Printed by
Berforts Group – Stevenage and Hastings
ISBN – 978-0-9575476-4-3

Dad 1957   *Doug Tucker 1987*

The company you keep shapes your destiny.

This book is dedicated to My Dad 'TED'
A man who lived his life congruent,
from his spoken word's to his actions.

Edwin Clifford George Tucker
Soldier, husband, father, legend
April 7th 1938 - September 21st 2013

Contents

People often say that motivation doesn't last. Well, neither does bathing – that's why we recommend it daily.

Zig Ziglar

INTRODUCTION

I didn't take the traditional route into sales. In fact, my early years were anything but what most people would expect. On leaving school at sixteen years old, I did several filler jobs until joining the Royal Marine Commandos to fulfil my childhood dream of becoming a soldier. In an early indication of the persistence and dogged determination that shaped my later career in sales, I tried not once, not twice, but three times to get through the gruelling induction training course required to get the coveted green beret.

My first setback came when I badly dislocated my right shoulder in a canoe surfing demonstration that went wrong. The injury took me out the game for eight weeks and, by the time I got back to the level of fitness required to return to mainstream training, I had to join a different troop. Not to be put off, I pressed on. Ten weeks after re-joining recruit troop number two, we set off on a six-mile speed march around the winding country lanes surrounding the Commando Training Centre in Lympstone, Devon. By the time I finished the run and got back to the 'grot' (dormitory), I was hobbling like a cripple. I took myself off to sickbay only to discover I had a very clean break in my left outside metatarsal, probably thanks to a combination of the weight being carried on the run and the way I had laced my boot. Looking back, I had thought it was uncomfortable at the time! There was nothing I could do to change it though and I faced yet another physical setback that would take ten weeks. So far, not so good.

For many people, these sorts of extreme setbacks would signal time for a rethink. I'm not just referring to the brutal world of Commando training, in which there is an extremely high drop-out rate indeed. I mean in any endeavour. Sales is a classic example. People join this industry with a dream of making it to the top and earning big bucks. Yet, when the reality of what is actually required on a daily basis becomes apparent, it is a complete shock and many simply opt out. They are not prepared to commit or to do what it takes. I think my experience in Commando training shaped much of what I subsequently did in sales, but more of this later.

The rigours of Royal Marines Commando training are obviously an extreme example of this tendency to give up when the going gets tough. The average troop of recruits will start about forty-five strong, yet only around five will ever finish with the troop they started with. Generally a further seven or eight will eventually finish when bones have healed. I was one of the eventuallies, getting there in the end, and it still ranks as one of the proudest achievements in my life.

On leaving the Royal Marines after a successful military career, I returned to Civvy Street and took a job as a firefighter. Although this public service offered the pleasing level of adventure and camaraderie I always crave, the salary on offer was not so hot. To make ends meet, I turned to various odd jobs until a chance meeting changed the course of my life.

While travelling in South Africa, I came across a new style of barbeque and was inspired enough by what I saw to persuade the somewhat cynical manufacturer of this piece of leisure equipment that I was the man to bring it to the UK. Of course, having secured this international distribution deal, this was the moment that I had to put what money I had where my mouth was and learn the sales business the hard way. Oh and that's not to mention the import business, distribution business, point-of-retail-sale business and the overall running of a bushiness business too.

The early days were tough and I was let down by numerous retailers who were happy to take the goods but less keen to pay up. After banging my head against what felt like a very hard wall for a while, I decided to rethink. The obvious answer was to sell my barbeques direct and cut out the (non-paying) middleman. So, that's how I ended up dressed up in a chef's outfit, dragging the barbeques around the pubs and clubs of the south of England in my newly leased white van. I enjoyed every moment of the experience, even though it was physically tough and I didn't help myself by setting gruelling targets, such as not allowing myself to go home until I'd sold six units. Even though I was completely exhausted by the end of each day, I always came home with a smile on my face thanks to my antics as the travelling barbecue chef. Indeed, it was in this period that I settled upon my lifelong mantra: have fun and make money.

It was another chance meeting, this time at the Ideal Home Show in London's Earls Court, that really took my sales career to a new level. I'd gone there to check out more opportunities for the barbeques and got talking to the owner of a home spa company. In passing, he mentioned the difference in the margins being made on our respective products and the penny suddenly dropped. He was making a small fortune on every home spa he sold and they were not going cheap. Ergo, the more expensive the item, the bigger the margin. If you want to make the big time, you must sell higher-priced items.

This was a turning point for me and marked the beginning of an increasingly lucrative career in sales as I targeted bigger and bigger ticket items to sell. In the ensuing years though, regardless of the service or product I was selling, I always kept to the core sales principles that I learnt on the way up. I work hard, pay attention to the detail, focus on my customers and always, always enjoy what I do.

Over time, I found my way into the financial services industry. Once again, I applied what I had learnt to this exciting sector and, sure enough, I enjoyed phenomenal results.

'This is fantastic,' I thought to myself. 'Everyone must be cleaning up.'

Except, when I looked around me, it became very obvious this wasn't the case. Many, many of my colleagues were struggling and clearly selling at a rate well below their potential. A lot were visibly discouraged and the drop-out rate of new advisers was noticeably high. Something wasn't right.

Intrigued, I began to look into this more closely. I quickly found my personal experience was being matched at financial organisations around the globe. Indeed, according to a 2011 study by Boston-based consulting firm Cerulli Associates, the number of financial advisers in the US had fallen to 320,378 at the end of 2010, from 334,919 in 2004. Some of that drop in numbers is down to the global financial crisis that hit in 2008, forcing many groups to shed jobs. There is also an element that, following that crisis, the whole sector rather lost its allure as a profession. After all, mention anything to do with banking at a dinner party and people start looking at you as though you are the devil himself. Yet, there is clearly more to it than that.

Getting started in sales, and in particular financial sales, is not easy. In fact, it can be really tough for the young and inexperienced. Not only do you have to be pretty nifty at sales but you've also got to be confident enough to get to know a lot of wealthy people and win their trust. In addition, you must convince them you know what you are talking about, that you understand the products you sell inside out and backwards and that you are working to their best interests. Oh, and you need to get them to like you enough that they introduce you to all their friends too.

Just to add to all this, anyone selling financial services today also has to contend with a whole bunch of new, sometimes very zealous, legislation governing the industry, all introduced in the now-very-cautious, post-credit-crunch world.

It's a tough business. This is why, when firms recruit up to two thousand trainees a year, they expect just a *quarter* of them to make the grade and become fully fledged financial advisers.

Right now though, the financial services industry is facing a bit of a recruitment crisis. It's a double whammy: young people are no longer flocking to the profession as they once were, and there is a high rate of leavers. This is fuelling a long-term problem of a desperate lack of good advisers, although you could also look upon it as a huge opportunity. Either way, the declining numbers of financial advisers will only accelerate in the next decade, as many brokers reach retirement age. The average adviser is currently forty-nine years old, with 14 per cent over sixty, which means the race is on to find younger, willing recruits. And therein lies the real challenge.

It is my firm belief the figures needn't stay this bleak. There are many more trainees who are capable of becoming successful financial advisers than who currently make the grade. Our industry doesn't have to 'put up' with losing so much of what should be a great resource. Retaining good trainees and developing them into top sales advisers simply takes a bit of training, effort and application.

I began training and mentoring sales people around fifteen years ago after colleagues encouraged me to pass on my tips for success in sales. They thought my energetic approach to getting and keeping new customers could really help people new to the industry. Or, maybe they just wanted to get me out of the office so I'd stop bouncing around and burbling on about all the ways we could make this process more efficient and a lot more fun. Either way, my motivation was to help others achieve those spine-tingling breakthrough moments when you just know that sales is the best career choice ever. Since setting out, I have helped hundreds of sales professionals at training and motivational speaking engagements around the globe. I've worked on a one-to-one basis, mentoring individuals, and have spoken to large groups on intensive two or three-day courses.

The inspiration behind my training programme is my

belief that there are a lot of parallels between a Royal Marine Commando and a sales professional. Both require discipline, training and dedication to the job to ensure they are always at the cutting edge and the best in their field.

If you are truly serious about rising to the top in sales, you have to train hard, work harder and fully understand your environment, just as I had to in order to gain my coveted green beret. It's not easy, but then nothing worth having ever is.

Doing well in sales isn't rocket science though. There are no complex formulas that will lead to guaranteed success. If you want to do well, you need to use your time efficiently, perfect a mixture of certain key skills and commit to giving your all.

To make things easier and help you reach the ranks of the sales elite – that is, to help you become a sales commando – I have devised a step-by-step training programme that I've outlined in this book. The chapters will take you through each stage of the selling process, from prospecting to setting up initial meetings to how to conduct yourself in those meetings. I've also laid out a number of powerful weapons you might like to use to get those all-important referrals, because it's a bit of a waste of time getting in front of people if you don't use the opportunity to get more contacts.

Many of these weapons will only take minutes to deploy, sometimes even less than a minute, and yet you'll get maximum impact. To prove it to you, I've timed some of the key responses that are shown throughout the book and added a note on just how quickly you can gain the upper hand.

Each one of these techniques will work in isolation and you will almost certainly see a rise in your sales statistics if you use just a handful of the ideas I give you. Incorporate them into one strategy, though, and your sales figures will go through the roof.

Of course, having mentored hundreds of sales people, I am more than aware that things don't always go to plan. Prospects are not obliging enough to follow a script, answering each question positively and then agreeing to sign without a murmur. No, prospects are human like you and me and, just when you think you're getting somewhere, they'll inevitably lob in an objection or two. Or, worse still, they'll suddenly say 'no' right at the end of the meeting, after nodding away happily all the way through.

What drives me to distraction is when a salesperson doesn't know how to deal with these wobbles and panics or, worse still, runs away. That is not the way of the sales commando, and that is why I have set out dozens of ways to see off objections, including many scripted set-piece plays for you to practice. And practice is the operative word here. Just like their Marine Commando counterparts, sales commandos need to be so well drilled that seeing off setbacks becomes second nature.

Know your objection set-piece plays like the back of your hand and nothing will ever surprise you.

Many of the lessons described in this book may seem completely obvious on first reading. 'I already work really hard,' you might say. But do you? Hand on heart, do you always pursue referrals with vigour? Do you always put every effort into going the extra mile? If you do, you are certainly the exception.

In my experience, salespeople rarely follow through effectively on their initial approaches, too often get distracted by definite maybes and even sometimes miss obvious buying signals from their prospects. Indeed, most of the salespeople I have come across in my years on the road are simply not trying hard enough. Or, they make the very amateurish mistake of thinking they are working their socks off while they are actually doing nothing useful at all to further their sales career. They completely fail to distinguish between being very busy and being very productive. The result? They don't make nearly as much cash as they imagined they would.

Whatever you do in life, if you want results – real, tangible, demonstrable, lasting results – you've got to work for them, but you've got to do the right thing too. Look at it this way: if you want to change your body and lose twenty, thirty or forty pounds of fat, it isn't simply a case of doing a bit of exercise here and there. For that sort of goal, you need to eat the right way, map out a suitable training programme and adjust it as you go along to reach your goal as efficiently as possible. Simply turning up and sweating a bit now and again isn't going to do it. If you don't want to waste countless hours of blood, sweat and toil on actions that are ultimately fruitless, or may even have a negative impact, you need to have an effective plan of action. Otherwise, you'll simply be a busy fool.

This happens all the time in sales. I regularly hear sales managers declare they are far too over-worked and busy. I often see managers who run teams of salespeople getting copied into each email that gets sent, or have people coming to them every ten minutes with some question or another, causing the slightly ludicrous situation in which their interruptions are interrupted.

It is madness. No salesperson should be spending their day firefighting. When we are firefighting, we are only ever going to be in damage-limitation mode and not in the all-important creation mode. Every one of us should strive to be leading at all times, with maximum efficiency and effectiveness, whether we are leading teams of sales professionals or teams of prospects and clients.

Do you know what happens when you don't use your time efficiently? You tie yourself in knots and end up in a never-ending loop of disappointment and damage limitation. Let me draw you a picture.

Imagine you are sitting in front of a prospect. In a desperate bid to get them to do business with you, you promise them unrealistic levels of service and ridiculous rates of return on their money. You are doing this because you've not put any effort into building up your sales muscles. Perhaps you've convinced yourself you simply don't have the time to put your back into the job or what you know already is enough. Or, maybe you blame your existing clients for your lack of time, because they are always complaining and demanding attention. Of course, this completely ignores the fact these existing clients probably have a very good reason to complain because you've previously promised them the Earth and have thus far delivered very little. And so the circle of discontent goes on, promise after empty promise. It perpetuates itself proportionally to your level of ineffectiveness and inefficiency.

Now, you can kid yourself this isn't you. But stop for a moment and ask yourself whether you've ever said something like this: 'But I work really hard. In fact, I see twice as many people as most of the others in my office and I'm not afraid of rejection. I just don't get it. I deserve better.'

If this is you, you *are* being a busy fool. To be blunt, unless you stop kidding yourself and put some effort into creating a more effective sales system, you don't deserve to make money.

Busy doesn't mean a thing. Busy is nothing, productive is everything. Busy *and* productive co-existing is *domination*!

The secret to getting your day, and therefore your career, back on track is to adopt an efficient sales system and then give it your all. Use this guide to analyse your sales processes right the way through, then refine and perfect them, so each one of your skills is used to the optimum capacity. Get to know your set-piece plays so you really do have an answer for everything, and that answer will be convincing because it will be utterly in line with your values and beliefs. Then, put all your undoubted energies into making it work again and again. Yeah, you'll be rushed off your feet, but you'll be busy making money, not empty promises.

This programme isn't an invitation to cut corners or to follow the path of least resistance. No. I expect you to work harder than you've ever worked before. However, the first, arguably most important, step towards becoming elite is to accept the way you are currently using your time may not be efficient.

To become a successful sales commando you need to develop deep, fruitful, long-term relationships with clients. 'Selling' does not just take place at the end of a transaction, when money changes hands. The process begins long before that final commitment and, if you handle it correctly, should go on a good long time after you've got the cheque in your hands. Long-term partnerships, repeat business and referrals, where both sides feel really good about working together, are the key to a successful and lucrative career in sales.

No one likes being 'sold to' and today's buyers are more sophisticated and knowledgeable than ever before. If they feel badgered or hectored, or that you are not on their side, rest assured that they will go elsewhere. No, the job of an elite salesperson is to motivate prospects into action. You won't ever do that unless you are truly in tune with what you are selling and have taken the time to properly understand your prospect's thoughts, desires and perceptions.

As you prepare for your new career as a sales commando, try to think of the system you're about to adopt as an engine. This engine will drive your sales and power your productivity. Clearly, that means the engine design is key. I'm not advocating re-inventing the wheel here. What I'm suggesting is a complete tune up, with maybe one or two evolutionary upgrades.

It helps to have a blueprint to guide you in con-structing your engine. The best way to start is to research the marketplace and look at the engines that are always way out in front, at the top of their field. These are the ones that are the most effective in terms of both fuel economy and power output. All you need to do, to replicate this success, is to tune your engine to these specifications. You may even like to design a hybrid that takes the best parts of the design from all the different engines you've observed. Don't forget, you are in control of this process. It's your career, your income and your life. It is up to you to make the process as effective, efficient and productive as it can be.

This book is here to help you in this endeavour. I have been travelling the world for many years, training and observing financial services sales professionals. During this time, I have worked with and observed hundreds of different engines. I've seen at first hand what makes one engine surge in front of the pack and what slows others down to a crawl. I know exactly what it takes to rise to the top in this very competitive world and I have shared my secrets in the chapters that follow.

To make it easier for you, I've interviewed a number of top sales professionals in our industry. These sales professionals operate at the top of their field, hailing from top financial firms around the world, and are the 'engines' that you should aspire to beat. They agreed to share their secrets to success in sales and their advice on how to make it to the top. Each chapter features tips and candid anecdotes from these legends in our industry. They've not held back in explaining exactly how their engines work and in sharing their stories of the journeys their engines have taken them on. Some of them have even been kind enough to admit to the odd screw-up and roadside fixes along the way.

Sales Commando is a practical guide. It will show you how to build relationships and how to deal with any reluctance on the part of the buyer. There are tips on how to qualify would-be clients and on how to order your own daily working schedule by setting meaningful goals. This book will show you the value of learning how to use your time efficiently and sticking to what you are good at.

Success in sales is not about a quick push and then sitting back to see what happens. It should be a way of life that is learnt, practised and constantly refined. This book will show you how, with some extra effort together with the benefit of some simple weapons, it is possible to become very successful indeed. Whatever your starting point or level of experience, you will get better at selling if you use this guide. I guarantee it.

My vision is for sales professionals to use this book to help them design their very own super-efficient sales engine. A domination machine, if you like. Design it, test drive it, tinker with it and then hone your skills to become elite.

Follow the advice in this book and the steps laid out in each chapter, and you will become the person that people look at and say, 'I don't know how they do it.'

Perhaps then, if you feel generous and benevolent and want to improve standards in your immediate environment, you might hand your new-found admirers this book. Tell your colleagues to read it too, because this is a good place to start a spectacular sales career.

Are you ready to find your own commando spirit?

Chapter one

GET READY FOR THE GAME:

the bench presses and squats of selling

If you have built castles in the air, your work need not be lost;
that is where they should be. Now put the foundations under
them.[1]

CASE STUDY
I was born to be in sales

My first sales job was in a non-commission industry selling cars. The sad fact was, some of the vehicles my firm sold were complete rubbish. Indeed, the only reason so many of these badly made cars came with an impressive five-year warranty was because they really needed it. They broke down all the time. I hated seeing people drive off after buying them and from the start I was brutally honest with everyone who came into the

---

1   Henry David Thoreau, author (1817–1862).

showroom. I always tried to steer them firmly away from the models that just weren't worth it.

I'd go as far as physically leading them in a different direction, saying stuff like, 'That Nissan will last you ten years, no questions, and it's £5000 cheaper than that piece of shit over there.'

Within just six weeks I became the top salesperson in the company, which put a lot of noses out of joint because I was only a kid working a three-day week back then.

One day, a little old lady came in with her husband and I did my usual thing, giving them a pretty honest appraisal of the various options on offer. We all ended up going for a test drive in a Nissan, the lady in the front, her hubby in the back.

'What do you think of this one, Chris?' she asked.

'I think it's a great car and it has only done 10,000 miles,' I said with complete truthfulness.

They seemed quite satisfied and when we got back they asked me to appraise their Proton for its trade-in value. I was frank with them that they weren't going to get an awful lot for it, but I did my best to give them the best price I could.

One week later, the lady returned to the garage with a Tesco carrier bag stuffed full of cash. It's true, there were notes bulging out of the side.

She just walked in and demanded: 'I want to see Chris Withers.'

My boss came hurrying out to get me and said, 'The

impression you made on her was fantastic. She wants the Nissan and she wants to pay cash. She's asked for you to personally deliver it to her house.'

Of course, I went over there and ended up staying for over an hour, drinking tea, eating biscuits and hearing about her kids and grandkids. Eventually, I had to politely tell her I really had to go back to work.

'Right, well I really want to give you something extra because I know you don't get commission,' she said, pressing £3 in coins into my hand. 'Buy yourself a pint love.'

I was a bit taken aback and said I couldn't possibly take her money. Do you know what she did? She made her husband lock all the doors. She wouldn't let me leave her house until I'd accepted the cash. I laughed a lot that day.

That was the moment I realised how much I loved selling. In fact, if you are good at it, it isn't even selling anymore. It's just helping people, and what could be more pleasurable than that?

Chris Withers, Area Manager

When I passed my final Royal Marine Commando test all those years ago and was awarded my green beret on the windswept landscape of Dartmoor, my overriding feeling was one of love as I pulled that piece of cloth onto my head. In that symbolic moment all memories of the physical and mental pain I had endured to reach that achievement faded into the background. Yes, my limbs still ached and I was vaguely aware I was on the brink of exhaustion after thirty weeks of the most gruelling endurance tests and virtually no sleep, but that really didn't matter. I had done what I had set out to do. I had achieved my dream.

As a Commando, you do what you do not because you are *made* to do it but because you *want* to do it. The sacrifices you make are made through desire. My ultimate goal was to be a Royal Marine Commando and I was prepared to go through anything to meet that aim. The reason I pushed myself well beyond the stage where most people would give in was down to that sheer passion, ambition and depth of emotion. That is how I achieved my dream.

There is a lesson there for us all. The first step towards becoming outstanding in any occupation is to be totally in love with it. It doesn't matter if you are a Royal Marine Commando, salesperson, sportsperson or art historian; if you don't love what you do and live and breathe it to the depth of your soul, you'll never, ever be the best. You may be able to bump along if you've got some raw talent, but you'll never achieve your full potential. You'll never experience that feeling of pride that you get when you know for sure that you've stood head and shoulders above the rest. And that, team, is how a sales commando should always be feeling.

If you want to get to the top and be the best of the

best, you've got to *fall in love* with sales. To become a true sales commando, you have to find a level of intense passion and commitment about what you do that soars above that of everyone else. It's that depth and intensity of feeling that produces outstanding results, often in the face of impossible odds.

This shouldn't be too tough either. Selling really is a *beautiful* profession. If you are at the top of your game there is no feeling to match the buzz you get when you close a sale. Even better, you can experience this buzz day after day after day. If you have chosen sales as your career but have never really thought that hard about why, it's time you woke up and started seeing it for what it is. Once you view it clearly and understand what you are truly gazing upon, you won't be able to help falling in love with it.

Without exception, all of the most successful salespeople I have observed while in their flow have a manner and bearing about them. They have a certain way of being, a passionate belief in their job. They really do seem to light up when they are working. They fill up with enthusiasm and energy as they go about their day because they are totally engaged and in love with what they do.

And guess what? People like this earn all the money. Really. It's a pretty well-known figure that the top 20 per cent of sales people earn 80 per cent of the money. I can tell you for a fact that that top 20 per cent *love* what they do with a passion bordering on the obsessive. So, if you want to become one of the highest-paid people in your profession and accelerate your career into the stratosphere, you'd do well to find their level of passion.

When you are truly in love with selling, it will shine out. There will be intensity about everything you do, from the moment you first speak to a prospect to the time they are signing on the dotted line. When you sit in front of that prospect, it will feel like nothing else in the world exists.

This is the level of total commitment I want for you when you view your place in financial services. It is this depth of feeling that will see you through the good times and the not-so-good moments when things don't quite go as well as you'd expected.

We all know and accept that few professions expose their recruits to as much rejection as the financial advice industry. Making it past the 'no' word, time and again, needs persistence and a certain resilience. Often, trying to push your way into something as personal as investments can provoke some harsh responses. But fear and not making enough contacts are what derail those people who don't love selling. These are people who will never cut it as sales commandos.

Sales commandos approach their profession systematically, relying on hard work, discipline and effective planning and organisation. They don't allow themselves to be stymied by sales shame because they are confident enough in what they do to know how to show the person in front of them that they can truly benefit from their services. They are that sure about what it is they do and how well they do it.

To begin your training as a sales commando, we are going to focus on falling in love with what you do and who you are.

> I love the hunt and challenge of the sale. It's an amazing feeling to use your knowledge to create really bespoke and ingenious solutions for people that perhaps other brokers don't see or really understand. The pleasure in the creativity of making sales in this way never ever wears off.
>
> *Andrew Oliver, Senior Area Manager*

Why sales is the best profession ever

If you do what you love, you'll never work a day in your life.[2]

Think about why you got into sales in the first place. Remember that drive and desire? What was it that attracted you then? Write down your answers. Can you fill up a page, or have you got a serious case of

---

2   Marc Anthony, musician (1969–).

blank-sheet syndrome? If you do, it's time to do some work.

Be proud of what you do, because you have chosen the absolute best profession, ever. Why? Well, here are four good reasons to start with:

1. *Income potential:* There are few careers that offer anything like the income potential of sales. Not all sales jobs offer an unlimited income – but many do.

2. *Flexibility:* You are the boss. Most firms are more than happy to let salespeople set their own schedule, as long as specified activities and training levels are met. Career freedom like that is hard to come by elsewhere.

3. *Job security:* Good salespeople are *always* the last to be axed from any business because cutting out your main income stream doesn't make sense if you want to keep the firm afloat. Even if the worst happens, successful salespeople are rarely out of work for long. Good sellers have tremendous market value. Plus, there is less competition for sales jobs. There are on average just 1.03 job seekers for every financial adviser post, compared to 9.22 applicants for retail jobs and 10.03 for would-be firefighters.[3] Who cares that shop staff and firemen don't see this opportunity – it leaves the way wide open for you!

4. *Emotional reward:* Everyone likes to think their job

---

3   Careerbuilder.com.

is important and serves a purpose, but how many can say they are emotionally rewarded by what they do? There is not much that matches the feeling of closing a big deal. Add in the fact that you are actually helping people and that's something to guarantee a satisfying working week.

Sales isn't a career with a single dimension, either. In fact, like any good, long-lasting true love, there are loads of different things to keep your interest day in day out, plus plenty of variety to keep you on your toes. You'll never, ever get bored.

Look at all these elements we use on a daily basis in our jobs:

» entrepreneurship
» psychology
» science
» art.

In fact, being in sales is like having several different jobs all at the same time. Each one of these elements listed here is part of being a financial adviser, wherever it is you work. Plus, each element has a multitude of aspects within it to keep you on your toes. It's almost impossible that you wouldn't find something of interest in your working day, and my prediction is that there will be enough to keep you stimulated for pretty much every minute.

Just look at those elements in more detail, if you are still not convinced. Thus:

» *Entrepreneurship:* Sales is the ultimate entrepreneurial profession. It has it all – the opportunity to self-start again and again with each new prospect, the freedom to create and think on your feet (occasionally in tricky circumstances) and a constant need for inventive marketing and promotional ideas to get your services into the minds of the people who count. These are not one-off skills either – you need to think like an entrepreneur every hour of every day. Figuring out the best approach is what you do.

» *Science:* Do you realise how much science your sales career involves? There is science in uncovering the gaps in your clients' financial lives and in constructing the most effective way forwards. You need to be an expert in the complete range of objective mathematical facts that are required to construct effective personal-life business plans to help your client set realistic financial goals. Don't worry though – no white coats are required.

» *Psychology:* Being able to gain rapid trust with another human being is not easy, particularly when they may be nervous, unwilling or unsure. Very few people are truly skilled at this and many salespeople struggle too. Mastering the ability to communicate on your clients' level and to motivate them into action requires a thorough understanding of human psychology. It's not one size fits all, either – even though they all have similar needs, every customer is different, in both their objectives and personality. You need to be able to adapt.

» *Art:* There is an art to the way good salespeople 'subjectively' design the solutions for their clients and an art too in creating the perfect fit between an individual and the solution to their problem. Salespeople who differentiate themselves from the rest in their creativity and flair win every time.

Being in sales is an awesome job where you, and only you, are in charge of your destiny. If you want to make more money, you can work harder, faster or smarter. You don't need to depend on anyone else because your ability to succeed (and by how much) rides solely on you.

You don't have to just take my word for it. With a job spec this good, not surprisingly, working as a financial adviser ranks as one of the best jobs *in the world*. Yes team, according to one survey, our profession ranked as the fifth-best career in a list of over two hundred jobs. The experts said we have less stress, a better working environment and fewer physical demands than most jobs.[4] But you probably already know that.

Don't forget either that, thanks to the impending retirements of the millions of baby boomers around the

---

4   CareerCast.com, 'Ranking 200 jobs from best to worst', April 2012.

world, we are in the very best place to be because many, many more people need us and will continue to do so. There is no question about that.

You get to meet awesome people too when you work in sales. Okay, not every client is going to become your best buddy, but you are *guaranteed* to meet some pretty amazing people in your line of work. I bet you already have.

Finally, my personal favourite answer to anyone who asks me why sales is just *the* best job ever is: you are always being pushed. If you work in sales, you won't ever experience that moment when you realise everything in your life is stagnating, or it all stinks, or is just dull, dull, dull. You won't ever suffer the same regrets as everyone else. A sales career, when done well, means your life is never ever going to be that way. Being in charge of your own destiny, you've got to make things happen all the time, every day. Goals are your bread and butter. Looking ahead, forecasting, predicting and planning are just small parts of the picture. Working like this is not just motivating and inspiring – it is exciting.

Sales really is an awesome job. So, relish what you do and you will naturally become so incredibly good at it that you actually love your own design and the way you deliver your craft. Once you are fully engaged you *will* lead the life of a passionate professional earning six to seven figures per year. What's not to love?

Within fifteen minutes of meeting someone, you've got to get them into a position where they bare their entire financial soul to you, so you can help them in a way that is meaningful and lasting to them and their loved ones. You've got to be able to show them things about themselves and their own personal finance that they never, ever knew. And these are things that are vitally important to them too.

It's a privilege to be able to do that. The biggest commodity any one of us has is our time and to spend it helping someone is a wonderful thing to do. The fact you can also be rewarded with a lot of money for doing that is the icing on the cake.

Noel O'Leary, Executive Director

100 per cent commitment

The quality of a person's life is in direct proportion to their commitment to excellence, regardless of their chosen field of endeavor.[5]

Of course, with any true love comes commitment and this undertaking is as important in sales as it is in relationships. The reason why so many people fail to achieve their sales

---

5   Vince Lombardi, coach (1913–1970).

goals is not because they are lazy, or lack motivation, or didn't put in the hours. It is because they were never *fully committed* to succeed. If you want to make things happen, you've got to buy into the process completely. There is probably not a single great achievement ever that didn't have a firm plan of action and then an unshakeable commitment to get it done.

I know some people find commitment tough. They like to think of themselves as 'free agents' and don't take to the thought of being tied down to anything, for any period of time. They prefer to keep their options open and reserve the right to pick things up and drop them again just as quickly if the mood takes them. Fickle folk like this will quickly move on if they see an opportunity to make a fast buck elsewhere.

That isn't you though. If you are reading this book, you want to be a sales commando. You already have a burning desire to be one in an elite group of top salespeople. If your goal is to join those elite ranks of sales commandos, you need to commit 100 per cent. Nothing less will do.

Commitment is the cornerstone of anything of value. Being committed to something means you truly value it. If you are totally serious about becoming the best of the best, you need to be completely on board. That means you will entertain no distractions or outside influences that might affect your performance.

If you want to become a sales commando and benefit from all the respect, admiration and power that go with that high status, you must be fully engaged and utterly committed to your profession as a financial adviser. To be a true sales commando, you must be totally sold on your products, your company and yourself – in other words, the advice you give and the way you give it. There can be no compromises.

The pressure will be unrelenting too because to get into that top 20 per cent – you know, the guys who grab 80 per cent of the action – you've got to commit to lifelong learning. The most valuable asset you've got is your mind. The more knowledge you have, the greater the rewards and the more you will be paid. That means you need to get out and attend seminars, watch podcasts and, of course, read books like this one. Know your craft inside out, backwards, forwards and upside down. Commit to getting better and better every day.

Knowing your market and products is *the* way to gain a prospect's trust and that is, of course, half the battle. Statistics show that 26 per cent of customers don't trust their financial advisers and that 18 per cent don't really know how the adviser can help.[6] With a hostile reaction like that, you've got an uphill struggle ahead of you if you haven't done your homework.

This commitment to the learning process is invaluable if you want to fall in love with sales. You need to understand every aspect of the subject so you can fully respect and appreciate all of its qualities. You must become fully absorbed in every facet.

6   IFA VouchedFor survey, '*How dark will it get before dawn?*', October 2012.

Don't worry; learning doesn't have to be dull. We're not back at school now. In fact, I guarantee we are going to have some fun in the journey to becoming a sales commando. Just remember, though, we're not messing about here. We're going to war with this and when you go to war you play to win and win. When you play to win, excuses are not acceptable.

The way a sales commando does business is devastating to anyone, or anything, that gets in his or her way.

The good news is, it's highly likely that, if you've set out to be one of the best, you've already got a can-do attitude. You instinctively know that, to get to the top, you've got to give it your all and commit 100 per cent. In fact, even though we are at the beginning of our training, you've probably already got the basics right there, in your head.

Now, all we have to do is turn that inbuilt passion and commitment into solid action.

BURN THE BOATS!

In 1519, Spanish conqueror and adventurer Hernán Cortés set out to overthrow the Aztec Empire. He was not the first to try this. Many other ambitious warriors of the time had cast an envious look at the golden treasures of this fertile land. However, the Aztecs had fiercely defended their country, aided by brave soldiers drawn from its six million plus inhabitants and their unshakeable belief in their powerful gods.

Cortés was a lesser nobleman and didn't have a huge

budget for his endeavour. Before he set out, he worked out he had enough money to fund just five hundred soldiers, a hundred sailors, sixteen horses and eleven ships, which didn't seem much to take on a foe as powerful as the Aztecs. Unshakeable in his conviction, Cortés interviewed each candidate for the voyage individually. He wanted to look into their eyes and see their passion and conviction before he chose the very best men for the job.

On the voyage over, a few of this hand-picked team began to have doubts, but Cortés managed to talk them around. By the time they were close to land, though, some more had started to become a bit jittery about the task ahead. But, once again, Cortés raised their spirits with a rousing speech.

Then, the Spanish conqueror gave his final order before the battle ahead: burn the boats!

The handful of soldiers now knew they had no choice. There was no escape route or backdoor out. They had to fight like their lives depended upon it because, in all truth, their lives did depend on it. So they did. The supposedly unconquerable Aztec Empire fell and Cortés was named as governor of New Spain, or Mexico as it is today.

That is what commitment and belief can do. What are the boats on which you float your excuses on a daily basis? If you torch those excuses, you will be engaged and will fight to win.

It's a lesson a modern sales professional would do well to learn.

Hand in hand with commitment are conviction and alignment. Let's take conviction first. The ability to be convincing has to be one of the key elements of a sales commando's armoury. If you can't convince someone, you can't gain their commitment. If you can't gain commitment, you won't sign any deals. Yet, you will never, ever gain commitment from a prospect if you have none yourself. After all, how on Earth could you possibly sell something if you yourself are not already sold on it? You wouldn't buy anything from someone whom you didn't believe, so you can hardly expect your prospects to overcome this crucial factor in human interaction either.

A true sales commando is *always* utterly convinced by what they do and that is how they get the upper hand. This means you have to be utterly knowledgeable about your subject and, just as importantly, totally sure of your skills. Even in the modern era, where information is available to all would-be clients at their fingertips via the internet, you need to convince them you know more about your products than anyone else on the planet. You need the depth of knowledge and passion to convince them you know what works, what doesn't and what is the best solution for each one of their individual needs. If you can do this, you are home dry. Knowledge is, after all, power, so relish the strength of your own self-belief. Your innate skills mean you are coming from a very strong place indeed.

As for alignment, well, think of this word in its purest mechanical form, where it simply means to be aligned, straight and in order. When constructing the solid foundations to build a powerful career as a sales commando, it is essential to get things in order. That is exactly what we are doing here, right now. In the coming chapters, we will dig deep into the mechanics of our industry.

Your mission is to get things straight, clean and aligned, and that is just as important as falling in love with your profession. If you don't, your sales strategy will be weak, unstable and easily toppled. You will have little or no power and all the passion in the world won't make up for those gaps.

A true sales commando needs total alignment in every aspect of his or her career. That means 100 per cent commitment to the profession and total conviction when you talk to customers.

Align your beliefs and abilities, be utterly convincing with every word and action that run through your body and soul, love your sales career with a passion and I guarantee you elite status in your industry.

Right now we are at the very beginning of what I promise will be an exciting and ultimately fruitful journey. We need to start by focusing on the very fundamentals of selling, and you will need to dedicate your working hours to reaching the peak of your profession. What I need you to vow today is that every day you will be utterly committed to your cause, speaking and acting with utter conviction.

What's more, I want you to love every single moment of it.

One day, when you look back at the hard work, blood, sweat and tears you've put into becoming one of the top 20 per cent, I want you to smile to yourself because you never even noticed the pain along the way. You were too busy feeling awesome because you've achieved the dream.

Only a few sales professionals are worthy of the title 'sales commando' – are you ready to join us?

CASE STUDY:
Be passionate about what you do – it sells

It's always easier to sell if you are passionate about the job and the product you sell. I learnt this from my very first job in car sales. I worked for Citroen and back then their biggest seller was the Xantia. It was a great car, but to me it was an old man's car. I was in my early twenties and I liked the sporty numbers like the Saxo VTR and VTS. The old guy in the corner was great at selling the Xantias because he loved them. He could talk for hours about the walnut dash, the softness of the ride and the great suspension. Me? I sold tonnes of the Saxo and pretty much no Xantias. I'd take people out for test drives in the Saxo and talk about how well it handled corners. I really was a Saxo lad. The reason I sold so many was because I was genuinely enthusiastic. That really does come through when you're selling.

Graham Bentley, Senior Area Manager

There is no passion to be found playing small – in settling for a life that is less than the one you are capable of living.[7]

---

7   Nelson Mandela (1918–2013).

Chapter two

LINING UP PROSPECTS

The only action is massive action.

Prospecting is, without doubt, the most important tool in your armoury. The difference between being able to prospect well or not is the difference between enjoying success in abundance or simply surviving.

If you don't take prospecting seriously, you're not taking your career seriously. Once you've mastered the ability to prospect, you will be able to organise yourself and your working day to get the maximum benefit out of every moment. You will be able to get the most out of every single opportunity, retaining all the essential information and nurturing it lovingly until it finally bears fruit.

There is a secret to good prospecting and it is based on pretty simple physics. The more work you put into it, the more prospects you get out. Then, the more prospects you've got, the more chance you've got of smashing your sales targets. And that is what this is all about.

Think about it in a different way. Imagine you're trying to power a car but you've put only a tiny amount of fuel in the tank. It would travel for a few miles, depending on its fuel efficiency, then stop. The more fuel you set out with, the more distance you will travel. Plus, to keep moving forwards on your journey, you will require a continuous supply of fuel to keep your vehicle travelling at full speed. It's the same with sales. If you have a narrow pipeline and a restricted flow of prospects, you will naturally achieve a lower number of sales.

To summarise: if your thinking towards prospecting is small and narrow, you'll never achieve your true potential as a sales commando.

It seems pretty simple, huh? Makes you wonder why everyone isn't raking in six or seven figures. It seems that most people just don't get it, though. Indeed, in all of the time I've spent with sales professionals, it has actually been quite rare to see salespeople really upping their game when it comes to prospecting. (Meanwhile they wonder why they never seem to reach their sales targets.)

In my experience, prospecting generally seems to fall into one of the following four modes of operation:

1. Retreating, running away, cowardly avoidance of anything that smacks of prospecting. This style is possibly caused by fear of rejection in some way, or complete incompetence, but either way it's a battle plan for losers.

2. Nothing, none, zip, nada, zero action, passive sit and wait. No effort expended whatsoever. Sometimes it's hard to tell whether this person is actually awake.

3. Average, mediocre, kind of trying, although with no real strategy. Occasionally though, there is a half-arsed attempt at things. This salesperson gives the impression of wanting to do something, but he's happy to put it off until another day.

4. Full-frontal attack mode, with a massive action plan. Everything this person does says, 'We are going to war with this thing, we have a strategy and a plan of attack and we are going to win!'

You probably know which one of these categories belongs to the elite, right? The guys in the fourth category have 'winner' written all over them. Conversely, even if you have all the luck in the world, working to the style of any of the first three is *never* going to amount to anything.

I'm guessing you want to:

» create a massive income
» pull ahead of the pack
» win the battle
» ensure further success
» become incredibly valuable to yourself, to your company and indeed to your family from a financial perspective.

If you want these things, you have to go into full-frontal attack mode. This means *huge, massive action*. To do this you need a strategy, a plan of attack and the absolute certainty you are going to win. You'll have to be trained, strategised, ready, willing, able, relentlessly aggressive and determined not to stop until victory is achieved. That's the true sales commando style.

Let's begin this section by being brutally honest about the prospecting level you currently favour. After all, if you know where you want to be, as a hugely successful sales commando, it helps to know where you are coming from.

Looking at the list above, which category do you currently fall in? To help you decide, I've expanded the styles a little below.

1. You regularly see some sort of opportunity yet don't do anything at all. When you do attend any event, which is rare, you feel uncomfortable introducing yourself or asking for a business card exchange and never, ever strike up a conversation unless someone approaches you first. Occasionally you have a good idea about how to meet prospects, but you've never followed through because you find it too daunting.

2. You attend what you call a 'networking event' now and again, but no more than once or twice a month. That is about as far as it goes though and you certainly don't have a prospecting plan, or indeed any kind of strategy to meet more prospects. If you were honest, you'd say you felt a little lost by the whole idea of prospecting.

3. You attend, or maybe even hold, some kind of event every couple of weeks on average, but again it is

not part of a formalised plan. Your career seems to go in fits and starts, where there are periods when things seem to be going well followed by long spells when it feels like you are stagnating. Often it is only when things go really downhill that you are spurred into making another push.

4. You've got a detailed written strategy for action, which you produce at the start of each year and update on a daily basis, marking off your progress and developing actions that have been particularly successful. It is quite likely you've found a prospecting style that suits you down to the ground and have regular events in the diary long into the future.

Don't be too hard on yourself if you currently fall in one of the first three categories. By being honest about where you are now, you have crossed an important hurdle. A key indicator that separates true achievers in life from the rest of the pack is that they are more honest with themselves. People who are destined for greater things don't have a distorted view of their own performance. Furthermore, they have high standards and constantly strive to achieve them.

Before you can get to where you want to go, you must understand where you are today. Having done this, you now have a good chance of navigating your way to your desired destination. It's in these small moments of life that the biggest differences are made.

So, take heart. At least we know where we are starting from and the fact you are reading this means you know the importance of style number four. In this chapter and those that follow, I will introduce some of the most successful prospecting styles you may like to try and will give you some advice on how to get organised and start prospecting the sales commando way.

It's time to go to war with this thing. A true professional won't be beaten down in any area. We will win the battle on all fronts and enjoy the spoils of our victory.

What is prospecting?

> I love talking to people and engaging with them. I think one of the things that works best for me is I am genuinely interested to hear what others have to say. That means it isn't difficult to get them to speak openly to me.
>
> *Noel O'Leary, Executive Director*

The number-one mistake made in prospecting is to confuse it with selling. Prospecting is not selling. In fact, if you are selling while you are prospecting, you are making a big mistake.

Correct prospecting is about exposure and about

forging new relationships each and every day. It is about investing your time into others, solely with the view of benefiting *them* and not necessarily benefiting *you* immediately. You are finding qualified leads that may buy your products and only when this process is complete should the selling begin.

If you are still not convinced, let me draw you a picture, because trying to sell when you are prospecting is like putting the cart before the horse.

If you placed the horse up against that cart the wrong way round, with its head facing the wagon, the horse could actually push the whole thing backwards. A horse is, after all, a big, powerful animal. Apart from being a bit daft to see, this would, of course, be an incorrect use of that mode of transportation. Indeed, inefficiently using the tools and power available would be a waste of everyone's time.

If you reverse it and make sure the poor nag is facing the right way then bingo, you're off. You will be able to load the cart with five times more product and the horse will happily pull away at the cart all day long. Best of all, it will be going where you want it to as well. It's all to do with using the vehicle at your disposal correctly.

Granted, we've all had the rather pleasant experience of making a quick sale after meeting someone socially. It feels great, doesn't it? However, don't confuse that with 'good' prospecting. You were just lucky enough to be in the right place at the right time within a handy social circle. This is a million miles from being the correct way to strategise and position yourself when prospecting day by day. Apart from the fact you'll run out of mates sooner or later, you are taking a very short-term view in a very long-term game. No, you need to get your prospecting horse facing in the right direction and pulling its weight in gold.

Oh, and while we are busting myths about prospecting, don't fall into the trap of thinking it is all a numbers game. The old-fashioned view is that success is all about creating a mountain of cold contacts. It isn't.

Quality must come before sheer quantity. We need to line up quality first, then quantity second. We will then have a mechanism ready to dominate. You need to find prospects that have the desire – and the means – to buy your products. There is little point, for example, expending all your energies on prospects who live in a low-income area if they can't afford what you are selling. That horse wouldn't just be facing the wrong way – it would probably be a donkey.

Prospecting is not a part-time job

Right now, you may well be wondering how much of your working week should be devoted to prospecting. My answer may well surprise you.

At least 80 per cent of your time!

If I haven't emphasised it enough already, let me do so again: prospecting is *the* key sales tool. It is critical you develop your prospecting skills if you want to increase your sales and achieve long-term success. The majority of sales folk spend far too little time on this essential strategy and it shows. The bare facts are as follows.

If you spend too little time prospecting you will never achieve the sales success you desire. You'll never make it as a sales commando.

To prospect effectively, you should go about each and every day like a true entrepreneur. The vast majority of your time – at least 80 per cent of your waking day – should be invested in yourself and your reputation. (Note that I am saying 'waking' day, not 'working' day. Prospecting should be top of your mind all the time. If you are awake, you are prospecting.) Your number-one goal should be to get anyone and everyone to know who you are.

I always remember this simple piece of advice I got from a very successful businessman I met at one particular Ideal Home Show in London. He said: 'Remember my son, they are either buying from you or selling for you.' The concept of opening your eyes to the fact that anyone and everyone can, in some way, be adding value to your business is a good one to remember when taking massive action.

If you are one-dimensional in the way you go about prospecting – for example getting someone else to cold call for you or focusing on passive leads that may or may not come from advertisements – you will, quite simply, only ever grow at the rate that someone else will be prepared to work and feed you.

Don't relegate prospecting to a quick hour last thing in the day or first thing in the morning, before you get down to the real business of selling. That is a complete mismatch of your time and will reduce your chances exponentially. Prospecting should take up a large majority of your day.

You need to put that leg work in if you want to create an abundance of leads and expand your prospects pipeline.

If all this is a bit of a revelation to you, you may now be thinking, 'Hang on a minute, I don't get paid when I am prospecting.'

Forget that thought. In fact, you had better get used to the fact that, in your new career as a fully fledged, successful sales commando, you will actually only be doing things that 'get you paid' for a *minimum* amount of time. Possibly as little as 20 per cent. Get the prospecting part right, though, and I guarantee that, when you do sit down in a sales meeting with your new-found flow of prospects, wow – you'll be really motoring.

I'm going to ask you to make a choice. It is a clear choice you need to take right now.

Is prospecting going to be the first thing you do in the morning, the last thing you do at night and pretty much all you do in between?

Are you going to give it at least 80 per cent of your

time and 100 per cent of your attention?

Do you truly believe that, without sufficient efforts in prospecting, you are going to fail?

If the answer to all those questions is most emphatically 'yes', then I'm glad to have you on board. Let's get started!

The Italian job

In business, much is made of the 80–20 rule and, for those who have been living on a desert island and have never heard of it, it may be helpful to start with a brief explanation. Italian economist Vilfredo Pareto devised the rule in 1906, after he noticed that 20 per cent of the pea pods in his garden produced 80 per cent of the peas. Inspired by the idea, he began to extrapolate it elsewhere. He surmised that 20 per cent of the Italian population owned 80 per cent of the land. In factories, 80 per cent of the production came down to the most productive 20 per cent of industrial units. Pretty much everywhere he looked, the 80–20 rule was proven.

The 80–20 rule, or Pareto's Law as it is also known, is still widely accepted in business. Over time, it has been modified here and there, occasionally being reshaped into 70–30, or 85–15, but the central argument has hardly changed. Whatever industry you hail from, it is more than likely the minority of your workforce and/or customers bring the majority of profits.

So, what does this mean to someone aiming to be

part of the sales elite? Well, it goes without saying that you are dedicated to being in the top 20 per cent of the sales rankings, turning over 80 per cent of the sales. In addition, as I've already shown in this chapter, you should be spending 80 per cent of your time prospecting. Yet, there are other ways this rule is applicable too, and they lie in the area of efficient time management.

Almost without fail, all of the sales consultants I have worked with find that 20 per cent of what they do has the biggest effect on the whole sale's process. Therefore, 80 per cent of their daily efforts simply aren't as productive. It's that 20 per cent that gets them paid. This phenomenon even includes the amazing individuals whom I have studied more closely and who have contributed towards this book.

Common sense says we should all be constantly striving to find and stay in that 20 per cent zone, perfecting the things that have the biggest effect on our business and that really do bring us more clients. It is to our advantage to work on the 20 per cent of actions that really matter to the prospect we sit down with. (This will be covered in more detail in Chapter Five.)

Inevitably, every hour in every day will be filled with something, and it's our job as sales commandos to focus on the 20 per cent of our actions that are the most effective rather than the 80 per cent that simply pad out the time.

We are all guilty of spending countless hours, days, months and even years following this pattern of time-wasting behaviour in our professional and personal lives. It may not be intentional and you may never have even thought about it, but it all adds up to the fact you are not being as effective as you could be.

Reading this book is a step towards eliminating those patterns and uncovering what really works for you, just as hundreds of other very successful boys and girls around the world have done. Shaping your day around productive patterns, rather than the patterns you may currently be running that really don't serve you, is the way forwards.

One of my favourite authors, Timothy Ferriss, wrote a whole book on this very subject called The *4-Hour Work Week*.[8] The book was a bestseller and deservedly so, due to its simple, pragmatic systems centring around efficiency and productivity. If you haven't read it, *read it*! (Have that one on me, Tim.)

So, be aware of Pareto. That old Italian guy's genius discovery is around you in every aspect of life, especially in sales.

The only action is massive action

CASE STUDY
If you want to be the best, up your work rate

After I left college, I drifted for a bit. A mate, who was a manager of the local Dixons electrical store, offered me

8   Timothy Ferriss, *The 4-Hour Work Week: Escape the 9-5, Live Anywhere and Join the New Rich*, Vermillion, 2011.

some part-time work.

I'd never really been in a working environment before, but I could see straight away that there was money to be made. I was gobsmacked that none of the other guys who worked there seemed to see it. For example, they made everyone take an hour for lunch, so off they would all go at 12:30 pm, just as it all got busy. I always took my 'lunch hour' at 9:15 in the morning to get it out of the way. Then I'd take the rest of the day all the way. I cleaned up. At that time the shop was doing £40,000 in sales and I was taking around £28,000.

I'd be running between customers all day, bang, bang, bang. Meanwhile, when the other shop assistants were around and made a sale, they wasted so much time. I'd watch them go to the till with their customer, help them to the car with their TV, or whatever they had bought, and then amble back in store. I couldn't understand why they did this. Dixons was a shop. We weren't seeking referrals or even repeat business, so what's the point? The customer doesn't give a shit about who puts the TV in the car. I'd just take the customer to the till, shake their hand and tell them if they needed anything else, the cashier would sort them out. Then, boom, I'd be off to the next one. No time wasting.

After a while, I was sent to spend a little time in other parts of the store, because the other sales guys complained I was doing too much on the big-ticket items like the TVs. One day I was stood manning the kettles and saw this guy wandering around. I asked him what he was looking for and he said he wanted a can opener. I teased him a bit, saying he was really splashing out and told him he should at least buy an electric one. I had to try to up-sell him a bit just for the sport of it.

We both had a bit of a laugh and then I spotted him looking over at the TV section. I knew I wasn't supposed to be over there, but thought, 'Sod it'. I told the customer I hated talking about can openers, so how about a guided tour of the store? Off we went, with me still holding the can opener he was buying.

I ended up selling him a 33-inch Toshiba TV with full surround sound, a DVD player, extra cables and an extended cover plan. I chucked in the can opener for free!

At this point I stopped and thought: you know what, I'm quite good at this. I know a lot of people would have said here's the £14.95 can opener, thank you and goodbye.

David Hughes, Division Manager

Okay, so you've bought into the 80 per cent figure, but now what? You've read about this 'massive action' I've been on about, but what does that actually mean in practice? How much action is enough to get a suitable reaction?

Whenever I am asked this questions at one of my seminars, I tell people to imagine the level of input they'd need to get a steady flow of good prospects – and then multiply that level by fifty. Yes, fifty times. If you want to be the best in this day and age, that is the level of total commitment you need when it comes to prospecting.

If you put in partial effort, you will get failure. If you're only able to commit to an average effort, you will gain poor results. If, however, you go for it with massive action – at fifty times the level you originally imagined – you will get exceptional levels of reaction to capitalise on.

Or, to put it more succinctly, you need to tackle this part of your sales career in true commando style.

What, though, if you think you've been working pretty hard yet don't seem to be getting anywhere? In your own mind, you've been putting in that massive action but it isn't bearing fruit. It's worth tackling this here and now, because this does happen and it is really demotivating to the poor salesperson who is putting in all the effort but not generating anything like the leads they'd expect.

It's a problem I've seen many times first hand while observing and mentoring sales professionals. You can spot almost straight away that these people work hard but have never really given much thought to what they do for either their successes or their failures.

The first clue lies in the mismatch between what the client and the consultant think. When I am doing one-to-one sales training, I often sit in at a prospecting event or consultation. It quickly becomes apparent to me when the would-be client is not fully engaged, or even interested in what the consultant is saying. Yet, later on, when I ask the consultant how they think the event went, their description of the initial meeting is often completely different from my observations.

'Yeah, I think they're really interested in doing something,' they'll say. Meanwhile it's obvious to me the prospective client has already disposed of the salesperson's business card and has resolved to ignore his calls.

One possible reason for this mismatch is that there are no hard and fast rules regarding the right and wrong ways to do things. It's not like learning to drive, where the laws of the land, or rules of the road, are right there in black and white and it's clear cut what is right or wrong. In selling, situations and personalities vary, so all aspects of selling, and indeed prospecting, can be very subjective. This subjectivity means contact between clients (or would-be clients) and salespeople is open to distorted opinions, so it is no wonder some sales professionals never fully achieve their potential.

To make your life a little easier, so you can more readily sort the good from the bad, I've listed what I call the good, the bad and the ugly of sales prospecting. It should give you some clues about what is correct action and what is incorrect, or insufficient, action (however much you believe the client is hanging onto your every word).

Let's begin with the ugly.

Imagine you are attending one networking event per week. The event will probably have been organised by someone else. You turn up, nibble on a few curled-up sandwiches, mooch about for a few hours and then give out your business card to a few random people before you speed out of the door.

There is no other way to put this: it's damn ugly and it is going to get you zero, zip, nada. 'Yeah,' you may well want to retort, 'Well it's better than nothing, Doug.' But it isn't. In fact, I'd far rather you went home and rehearsed your presentation or brushed up on product knowledge because it is not nearly enough action. Not even close.

You have no strategy. You are not trying hard enough. You fail and are not a sales commando. There, rant over.

Now the bad.

In this instance, you'll be organising a networking event of your own, once every three to four months, where perhaps you get thirty to forty decent people in attendance. The people who come along will be primed and ready to listen to your presentation or to attend an informal dinner and dance with one-to-one chats afterward.

This scenario is tricky. It is one where I'd like to recognise your efforts but, actually, I have to say, 'Nice try but still a fail, please go stand over there with the rest of the failures.' I'm afraid there is no room for delicate feelings in sales commando training. Either you make the grade or you don't. It's black and white and simple.

You are doing some good things, but it is not nearly enough. *Fail*.

And finally, the good.

The day of the 'good' goes something like this. Every day, the salesperson meets with and buys a coffee for *at least* two people who work in their area or local community. These meetings may be with people in the same demographic or in a non-competitive businesses. The sorts of conversations that go on are something along the lines of: 'I deal with a lot of high-net-worth individuals who could use your service and I was wondering how I could introduce your company's products/services to them? How can I help you here?'

The 'good' person will be a member of a range of sports clubs, community groups and teams. In fact, they won't just be a member, they will be the 'go to' person who organises things and keeps things on track. Everyone knows they put in the extra effort and will always, always go the extra mile.

A 'good' person will have a regular stream of seminars, events and meetings every single day. Not once a week, once a month or once a quarter. Every single bloody day. Most importantly, they won't be constantly spewing out sales messages to anyone who may or may not be listening. They'll be the one doing the listening and getting to know their prospects.

That's massive action.

In a moment we will go through, in detail, ideas for ways to get in front of people. Right now, what you need to focus on is perfecting your prospecting skills. You need to learn how to get the flow going outwards to maintain the momentum of that massive action.

From now on, any event you go to, you need to have a pre-rehearsed plan of attack, a strategy and a goal. Say to yourself something like, 'I'm going to engage in conversation with five or ten people, collect at least five or ten business cards and throw a verbal invite out to four or eight of those people.'

Rehearse that invite beforehand. Say something like, 'I often get a few key clients I look after together for breakfast, or lunch, a couple of times per week. I would love to invite you so you can meet some of them. They're great people and I think you'd benefit personally from getting to know them. You've got a lot of business interests in common. How about I invite you to one in a few weeks?'

Practice your approach so that when you get in front of people you are skilled at asking them the right sort of questions. This more empathetic approach will mean they will really want to spend time with you, talking to you. It will give them a compelling reason to respond to you and stick around. Ask them questions like, 'How can I help you?' 'What can I do for you and your business?' 'What can I do to assist you and help you grow in your company?' 'I work with a lot of high-net-worth individuals; how can I go about introducing them to you?'

Let them answer too. Good prospecting is not about barrelling through a script and never giving people a moment to respond. Listen to what they are saying to you, brainstorm with them a little, make some commitments and deliver.

Never, I repeat never, start by launching into a conversation along the lines of, 'Hey, what can you do for me?'

Prospecting is all about giving and, as we all know, it is only by giving that you will ever receive. Concentrate on building the foundations of a relationship before you start to construct the deal and try to close it.

Once you are familiar with what prospecting is really about, get into a mindset of marketing yourself and getting maximum exposure. I want you to start thinking about how you are going to tackle your new prospecting strategy. Think big; you are going to devote 80 per cent of your time to this and you need to make every moment count. Your target is for everyone in your territory to know you, think you are a stand-up person and speak of you positively.

Take massive action and you will gain the responses you desire.

> You have to connect with your clients on a social level to begin with. If you connect on a social level, all of a sudden you don't need to turn up in your suit and tie as a financial

adviser talking serious business. Suddenly you are more of a friend. It only takes me one social encounter to cast myself as a friend. If I meet someone outside work, I'll invite them around for a barbecue, or for some other social event. Then, when they come in for a review later on, I'll shake the guy's hand and give the lady a kiss on each cheek. It's no longer, 'I am the adviser and you are the client.' It's, 'We are connected.' They'll want to help you. How powerful is that?

Graham Bentley, Senior Area Manager

CASE STUDY
Find what works for you

I was never comfortable with cold calling, or power hours, or any of those ways to generate prospects. It just wasn't for me. I'd rather have a game of golf, or football, or rugby. So, I'll be out every night, either playing or going to social functions connected with the clubs I joined. I've got to know loads of people that way.

Occasionally, I get someone who'll say they don't like the company I work for. They'll say they've read bad things on the internet, or heard something they didn't like. If you've got to know someone beforehand, though, and had a good time with them, it's easy to deflect anything negative and set the record straight. You can say something like, 'Well, there are fifty brokerages all over this country, but there are only three of us in the office here and we've never had any complaints.' The personalised touch makes all the difference. It will put their minds at rest.

You can close out the negativity by saying something like, 'I'll give you a shout on Monday, we can get a coffee and I'll tell you exactly what we do.' Then you go back to your golf and you know you've done your bit. You've got a good prospect all lined up.

Steve Rigby, Divisional Manager

Rapport and softening them up

This section covers positive salescraft techniques that can be utilised while prospecting *and* also in more direct sales meetings.

Before we get down to it, let's pause for a moment to explore a few bonus exercises that will help you as you prepare for the major attack. These are tried and tested techniques to build rapport and soften up your prospect before you deliver the *coup de grâace.*

The purpose of rapport is to relax a prospect sufficiently so they feel, to some degree at least, you are talking to them as a friend and not as a businessman. What do I mean by this?

Visualise meeting up with a good friend for a coffee.

This friend has a reasonably good job and maybe you haven't seen them for a month or so. Picture their facial expressions, how they hold themselves and the pace and tone of their voice. Focus on their whole demeanour and how animated this person would be as they told an interesting story about the events of the previous month.

Now picture a meeting with a businessman who you don't really know. Imagine him in an important negotiation. What does he look like? What are his facial expressions and how does the tone of his voice strike you? What are his overall posture and body language saying?

The chances are, you will have concluded something a little like this.

The businessman thinks and assesses words in a deep and thoughtful way. He looks, at times, quite stern and is a little guarded or defensive in his manner. When he speaks, he asks open questions and tries to steer the conversation in a certain direction. You get the sense he is protective of some information, almost playing poker with certain elements. He will constantly test the authenticity of what he is being told, often with some kind of doubtful overtone. In a nutshell, this person takes an offensive stance at times and a defensive and retracted stance at others.

Meanwhile, the friend is more likely to be open faced and happy, freely sharing conversations, stories and historical events. They'll have no qualms about asking for your advice or seeking council on certain subjects. They will be intensely interested in certain things you are saying. They'll be warm and accommodating.

Why do these two people seem so different to you? Well, we all assume different states and demeanours and process things differently depending on our physical conditions and state of mind. This, in turn, is dependent on the environment we are in at any given moment. It's rather like an actor getting into character. We assume a character we believe is appropriate for the occasion, whether it is relaxed and informal or businesslike and emotionally remote. The friend in the example above could very easily be the businessman on another occasion, it's just that the character he's chosen to reveal to you is his calm and spontaneous one.

Rapport is about creating the right environment – one in which a feeling of trust, mutual commonality and respect is formed regardless of the character the prospect has chosen to assume. You want to talk to someone who is in this open state of mind, as opposed to someone who is in business mode, when you are selling and providing advice. The former is obviously far more productive than the latter. In fact, the key to rapport is to make your prospect comfortable so they come out of character, and don't ever give them the opportunity to withdraw into a character that's difficult to connect with.

I must, however, add a word of caution here. Don't attempt to shoehorn your businessman into best-buddy mode. Premature overfamiliarity, indeed any overfamiliarity, breeds rapid contempt. Never, ever bound into a meeting back-slapping and hugging your prospect as though he is your long-lost best pal. You need a careful strategy to get this right.

To begin with you must consider your own character, as well as that of your prospect. When we switch into financial adviser mode we can, albeit inadvertently, enter a more businesslike state. Funnily enough, by doing this, we encourage the client to mirror that behaviour.

There are certain things you can do to start off on the right foot and they don't require any drastic changes. I always begin my seminars by saying to always take the easy way, and this certainly applies in this case. If you want to create almost instant (and positive) rapport:

» Dress for success. Think carefully about hygiene and cleanliness. Don't overdo the cologne and, if you smoke, don't go to a meeting stinking of cigarettes.

» Do your homework. Do your research and due diligence on the prospect, covering their profession, the company they work for and themselves.

» Be logical and interesting. Rehearse interesting opening questions that make sense and that can be delivered in a logical order. Stories and set-piece plays about yourself, from both your professional and personal life, are great icebreakers.

» Have a plan B. Plan a system that you can fall back

on if things are not naturally flowing as organically as you would like.

» Find common ground quickly. 'Me toos' are an easy way to find common ground. Whenever you spot an opportunity, flag it up with phrases such as 'me too', or 'yeah, that's like me' or 'I totally agree', or the good old 'I'm the same'.

When we have true rapport with a prospect, we are happy and comfortable with them. In turn, they will have trust for you and your advice. To keep you focused, make a mental note of this handy sequence of three steps. When it comes to human behaviour, people:

» *like* people first
» *trust* people second
» *do business* with people they trust third.

If you cast your mind back, you'll realise this sequence of three is evident in every deal you've ever made. To be successful, you need all these things and you need them in that order.

Stay relaxed but not over-familiar and never lose sight of your two most important objectives:

1. for your prospect to become your client
2. for him or her to positively refer on his colleges and friends.

I love structure and process, so everything I do has a structure, including rapport. In rapport I break my questions down into three different areas:

- present
- past
- future

I ask loads of open questions, such as:

Present: 'So, tell me a bit about yourself. What are you doing here? How long have you been here?'

Past: 'Okay so where were you before this? What's the history? What did you do in the past?'

Future: 'Now what about the future? Where do you want to be in five years' time?'

They love the future part because it's all about plans and achieving them. It's about results.

Alternatively, and depending on the type of person, you can encapsulate the whole thing in one question: 'Look, I know nothing about you really and part of my job is to get to know you. I really enjoy learning about people, so tell me all about yourself.'

And they just open up.

Andrew Oliver, Senior Area Manager

Body language is an enormous subject but it's worth spending some time on highlighting its importance in the whole communication rapport and selling process. There are so many massages that we all give off at any one moment and most of these signals and messages are not verbal.

I have always been aware of the importance of body language as a professional and the subject became even more apparent to me when I met Peter Collett, the Oxford don, eminent psychologist, author and TV personality who specialises in body language. Peter has presented a number of TV shows on body language, including *Body Talk* for Channel Four and *How to Get What You Want* for Sky One, and is also the author of a number of books including *The Book of Tells.*[9] I worked closely with him in 2011 on a project to assess how financial services sales consultants handled themselves in meetings and how they could do this more effectively.

The core conclusions from this were:

» All salespeople would benefit from being as visual as possible and backing up as much as they can with pictures and visual evidence.

» Create a shared space for the both of you when you meet, not too close and not too far away. The best responses were observed when a consultant was not sat directly opposite his prospect but rather

---

9   Peter Collett, *The Book of Tells,* Bantam, 2004.

slightly to the side, or off centre. As a rule of thumb, you should sit close enough to be able to lean forwards and touch the prospect but not so close as to be able to just lift your hand and touch them.

» What you do with any stationery, forms, notepads, iPads and diagrams is critical. Ensure any such interaction is done in a very sharing, demonstrative way. Everything you write should be able to be seen clearly, if desired, by the prospect. Don't adopt the stance of an interviewer and interviewee, with a clipboard held back on which you secretly take notes.

» Write down anything in such a way that the writing is large, bold, expressive and interesting. Where possible, visually demonstrate, prove and back up everything you say.

It will be more than worth your while to keep these points in mind while you master all verbal and non-verbal communications. You will be amazed at the level of rapid trust you will produce with everyone you meet.

EXERCISE
Body language

It should go without saying that you should ensure you watch your own body language. Little things make all the difference – for example, shaking your contact's hand with your palm up, not down in a dominating manner, and ensuring you not only listen but also actually appear to be listening. It should also be obvious that you shouldn't spend time checking your watch, or smart phone, during a meeting.

When it comes to *their* body language, here are some key cues to familiarise yourself with:

- *Crossed limbs:* indicating protective, defensive and guarded feelings.
- *Reduced smile:* indicating a business state of dominance and authority. Men in particular will reduce their smile, narrow their eyes and lower their eyebrows in a sign of authority and dominance.
- *The chin jut:* not only a sign of confidence but also of superiority.
- *The chin tuck:* an indicator of doubt; the prospect may even feel physiologically threatened.
- *The head tilt:* tilting the head to one side indicates vulnerability. It is also a good sign of trust and open listening.
- *The knuckle push:* presenting the back of your hand when gesticulating is a signal of forceful intent.

Memorise these cues so that, when you see them in your prospect, you instantly know what they are subconsciously telling you.

My final point on the subject of softening up your prospect is to remind you we only ever get one chance to make a first impression. You may be thinking, 'Yeah Doug, I get that,' but let me emphasise the point by sharing some research.

Princeton University psychologist Alex Todorov and his co-author Janine Willis conducted a study with two hundred students in 2005. They found definitively that snap judgements on character are often formed with insufficient time for rational thought. Amazingly, research subjects could predict with 70 per cent accuracy who would win an election after viewing a series of videotapes of politicians for microseconds. The scholars proved we form very firm and lasting opinions on people in fractions of seconds.

To summarise, the key aim in rapport is to show them that you *care*:

» Conversation: Have a conversation, don't give a lecture.
» Ask questions: Make these decent, open questions that are relevant.
» Relate: Relate to the prospect as often as you can.
» Enthusiasm: Be enthusiastic about the information they are sharing with you.

Make a battle plan

EXERCISE
Leave the business card at home
Most people attending a prospecting event, whether

someone else's or one they've organised themselves, go there with the intention of giving out as many business cards as humanly possible. Many even try to tip the odds in their favour by leaving piles of the damn things on every surface imaginable. Every time I've been to one of these things, you can't move for business cards sloshing about.

What's the point, though? Everyone ignores them and, even if you do manage to push one into someone's hand, they'll probably never look at it again, or it will be chucked in a drawer with all the other random cards they've picked up. Your phone will never ring as a result of your card exchange.

Relying on business card swaps is not the sales commando way.

In fact, next time you attend an event where there may be prospects, I want you to leave *all* your cards at home. Your new strategy is to take charge of all future communication and contact. You need to get the details of the people you speak to.

You may feel a bit awkward at first, having relied on the card exchange for so long. So, try saying something like: 'You know what, I've just given my last card away. Why don't you give me yours and I'll make sure you have an email with all my details on it within twenty-four hours.'

If they respond, bingo. It will open the way to other pre-arranged, pre-rehearsed questions in a rapport-building, information-gathering process. Once you've got their card, be sure to spend a few moments making some kind of memory-jogging note about them and your conversation. If you have a particularly successful evening or event, it's very easy to tell yourself that you will remember everyone clearly, only for it all to be a little mixed up the following day. Write notes on the back of the card, so the next day you just need to turn the card over and there is everything you need.

The most important detail to remember, though, is that it's far more effective to take charge of the communication by gaining a prospect's details than it is to give them yours and hope for the best. Always tell the new contact you are going to contact them, not the other way around, and, of course, make sure that you do exactly that.

Now you've resolved to devote time and energy to prospecting, you need a plan of action. You need a battle plan. In the next chapter, I will give you some ideas about the strategies you may like to try. Some may work well for you, others you may not find so effective. Some ideas may even be totally ineffective in your own case.

That's fine. Even though it takes a bit of trial and error, if you put in the effort, you will discover what suits you. The important part is not being afraid to try. Don't be put off from giving your all because you may fail. After all, when you are in full attack mode, some things will go wrong. There is no doubt you will suffer some collateral damage. In fact, if you don't, you are not trying hard enough.

Never be afraid of making mistakes. Hey, it's by making mistakes that we learn.

And, because you're going to do something every day, you're going to learn each and every day. Eventually, with this sort of input and momentum, you are going to hit upon strategies that work perfectly for you. These are strategies that will, without doubt, fit with you and your character type.

Once you've uncovered these methods and know what works for you, repeat the hell out of them and go on doing so until they stop working. If they ever stop working. Then, if the momentum slows, start experimenting with new, inventive ways of shaping things. Find different ways of gaining interest and helping people. Explore everything. Yes, it will be hard work keeping ahead of the game, but no one said it was going to be easy.

In fact, I personally don't want earnings of six to seven figures per year to be easy. Earning six- and seven-figure incomes isn't allowed to be bloody easy.

As a great mentor of mine once told me, 'Selling is the highest-paid hard work and the lowest-paid easy work there is!'

Get out there, work hard – ultra hard – every hour

of every day and the rewards will come back to you in spades. Attack the industry. Dominate your marketplace. Go to war with this and you will find victory.

You need to be trained, strategised, ready, willing, able and relentlessly aggressive, and don't even consider stopping until victory is achieved.

Chapter three

PROSPECTING

The full-frontal attack

Get in the zone.

Team, this is not get rich quick; you have to commit fully because we've got a lot to do.

In this chapter I am going to describe three hugely effective, attack-mode prospecting techniques, *plus* I am going to show you exactly how to get the most out of cold-call telephone work. This is by no means an exhaustive list of ideas for filling up your sales funnel, but it will give you a fair snapshot of what you should be doing to generate activity. You may like to adapt these ideas to your own style or to develop techniques of your own. The important thing is to start taking prospecting seriously. Right now.

Before we begin in earnest, though, let's talk about getting into the zone. It doesn't matter if it is face to face or over the phone, if you approach prospecting in a lacklustre way, you *will* fail. You have to attack each event, social occasion or call like you're tackling someone in a game of rugby. Keep focused on your desired target all the time and don't hold anything back.

If you want to be in the right place mentally at the right time, you have to be aware of all the signs that you are not 100 per cent focused. Work on finding some physical or mental exercises that you can use to pump you up whenever you don't feel in the zone or you feel a bit lethargic. It doesn't matter if this means dropping and giving me twenty push ups or giving a primeval yell at the top of your lungs. If that's what it takes, that's what it takes.

Be prepared at all times and, of course, remember rejection and the word 'no' are just part of the job of a sales professional. Don't let them send you off track or knock you down because there will always be people who say no. Instead, use any negative reactions to feed your hunger for finding a positive outcome. Let the naysayers make you stronger.

Make sure your subconscious is on side too by mentally rehearsing any objection you might come up against. That way, when you go live, you'll be ready for the game and you'll be able to smoothly and efficiently see off any reservations without missing a beat. Impressive, huh?

Maintain that positive attitude at all times by constantly focusing on your successes. Revisit in your mind every time you made a successful call or deftly handled an objection or made a prospect laugh, especially if only a minute before they'd been speaking to you in a very defensive way. Remind yourself how you felt when a prospect gave you permission to get in touch.

Each one of these successes will contribute to tipping the balance between having a confident spring in your step or dragging your heels throughout the day, wishing it would end. No one wants to meet a salesperson who hates his life, let alone trust him with their hard-earned cash. Get your head up, be positive and be fired up for the full-frontal attack.

You and only you are in control of your successes, your attitude and how much you enjoy your job. So, are you fired up and ready to nail prospecting?

Let's get started.

Working the phone

As soon as the fear approaches near, attack and destroy it. [10]

If there is one big secret to success for successful telephone prospecting, it has to be organisation and preparation. If you want to do it the sales commando way and join the elite, you've got to be ready for anything. Check and double-check everything. Then do it again.

Don't ever lose sight of the fact that the effort you put in will be directly proportionate to what you get out. Your skill level and sales process aren't an alchemy machine. Sadly, they won't turn crap into gold.

---

10   Chanakya, Indian politician (350–275 bce).

But you do have the opportunity to do something pretty spectacular.

Your attention to detail should begin long before you pick up the receiver. Obviously, you should start with a decent list, and there is some advice on this in the next chapter. I see far too many people struggling with prospect data from poorly researched sources. This is not the sales commando way. You need both quality and quantity to be a successful sales commando. Spend some time making sure your data is decent.

Next, when you are collating your data, invest some energy into putting it into demographic groups. Make a separate list for each definable demographic. Thus, construction workers, teachers, business people and so on all get their individual groups. The reason for doing this is for what I call the 'morphing effect'. This rule takes full advantage of the fact that, when you talk to specific groups of people, you will naturally adopt selling techniques that suit those particular groups. You may not even realise you are doing it, but believe me you will be.

Don't worry. I'm not suggesting you have a completely different presentation for each group, simply that you target each sector one at a time. If you call thirty teachers in a row, you will naturally adopt a style that will be more effective with that demographic, so it makes sense to concentrate your fire in their direction all at the same time.

The final, and arguably most important, part of your

preparation is to train, rehearse and drill yourself so you are in perfect shape. When I tried out for the Marine Commandos, I spent months training and getting myself in tip-top condition for the rigours ahead, both physically and mentally. You should be taking your sales commando preparation no less seriously. Take full responsibility for your presentation. Rehearse various ways of saying the same thing so you can appeal to many different character types, because not everyone is the same.

Be a master of your craft.

It doesn't matter if you're new to the industry or a veteran with twenty years of sales experience under your belt; you still need to prepare and train. No one is perfect and we should all strive for perfection every day. Role-play every scenario as many times as you possibly can and then do it that many times again.

EXERCISE
Getting through the gatekeeper

If the number you have isn't a direct-dial or mobile, the chances are you will encounter a professional gatekeeper, who is trained to stop you in your tracks. There are ways around this, but this is a perfect point to remind yourself of your mission objective, which is to have a good conversation with, and gain the interest of, your primary prospect. Evasion tactics are what's required. Here are some to try.

Intelligence

Good intel is essential for a successful operation in any field, and particularly in sales. The more you know about a prospect, the company they work for and perhaps even their competitors, the better. Clearly, the internet will hold a host of valuable information, so that is a good starting point. Personally, I prefer a more direct approach. Posing as a customer will allow you to talk to the gatekeeper, as well as different departments. Your objective is to get the full name, position and direct-dial number of the person you want to call. If possible, use a different phone, or phone line, for this approach. (While you are about it, don't forget to get the names of as many other potential prospects as you can along the way.)

Early bird or night owl?

It is a fact that the bosses and top earners usually get into the office long before the receptionist or gatekeeper and will often stay a lot later too. So, if you have no other options, call the number very early or very late. Chances are, someone other than the gatekeeper will answer the phone. If this is the case, act surprised and ask for the person you want to speak to.

Higher or lower?

Departments within a company often have telephone

numbers that are a digit different from the main telephone number. For example, if the number you have takes you to the switchboard, change the last number from, say, a 4 to a 5, and you'll often find it will take you to another department within that company, where you can ask, by name, for the prospect you are trying to contact. Sound surprised when they inform you that you are through to the wrong department and then ask to be transferred directly or prompt them to give you the prospect's direct-dial number.

When I first became a financial adviser, I really struggled on the phone, mainly because I put on this posh accent. I used to say things like, 'Hello, it's Graham Bentley. I'm just on my way to our appointment at 6 o'clock.' I remember one of my colleagues saying, 'What the fuck are you doing? Why are you talking like that?' I said, 'But I'm supposed to be a financial adviser.' I honestly thought the posh voice gave me authority and gravitas. The guys around me said I'd be much better off being myself and they were right. Now it's just, 'Hi, it's Graham, I'm on my way. I'll see you in a sec.' It makes everyone feel much more comfortable.

Graham Bentley, Senior Area Manager

Now we come to the call itself. Remember, you have your researched data, your sales funnel is full of gold, you've rehearsed your presentation and know backwards, forwards and sideways how you will overcome any objection laid before you. Your attitude is good, you're in the zone and you are ready.

You are through to your prospect and it is time to turn the sales commando machine on.

What happens now? Well, however you verbalise your presentation, the cold sales call will go through three main phases. These are:

» the introduction and permission
» the question and short story
» the close.

That is it. To make this a bit more interesting, let's play a game.

Picture each phase as a base in this game of sales, with the objective of the game being to take as many bases as possible in order to score maximum points. The rules of this game are quite simple:

» First base, the introduction and permission phase, is worth two points.
» Second base, the question and short-story phase, is worth a further three points.
» Third base, the close, is worth a whopping six points.

To clarify, let me map out exactly how you score. If you dial a number and the primary prospect answers and says 'Hello,' then boom, you've touched base. Give yourself two points even if you don't get any further than 'Hello, my name is...' (Did you hear that applause?)

If you get all the way through your introduction and gain permission from the prospect to talk for longer, then you've touched second base. Well done. Give yourself three more points. Once again, it doesn't matter if you get shut down immediately after the first word of your question; you've still arrived at second base and you've still earned your three points. (I'm definitely hearing a few cheers now.)

You can progress through second base by asking questions and fitting your services to the answers, all the while making everything you say personalised and relevant to the prospect. (Can you hear the crowd starting to roar?)

Finally, if you then ask a pre-closing question along the lines of, 'You would look at it, wouldn't you?' and you get even so much as a grunt of affirmation, or even better a full-blown 'Yes,' then it's time to leap off second base and steal third with an alternative-choice close. (The stadium erupts...)

> **You:** 'Are mornings, afternoons or evenings good for you? I have space on Wednesday at 10am, Tuesday at 12, or shall we say Thursday at 3pm?'

When giving an alternate-choice close, or indeed using alternative choices in objection-handling, always try to give three choices and not just one or two. Two options are an ultimatum, while three options is a real choice.

Once again, it doesn't matter if you get shot down at this stage. You've still offered a close and touched third base, so you still walk away with those six points. Take a bow. You're amazing. The crowd loves you.

At the end of the day, add up your points. The more points you have, the more appointments you'll have. It is that simple.[11]

To close this section on telephone cold calling, let me briefly touch upon words and tone. As professional persuaders, the words we use are our ammunition. Obviously, a sales commando should only ever use the best ammunition and never waste a shot. Using the correct dialogue, with perfect delivery, is critical if you want to hit your targets. We all need to use positive words, strong, open questions and robust statements throughout our presentations. Most importantly, you should strive to listen more than you talk and to make everything you say as relevant, logical and easy to understand as possible.

The other weapon you have at your disposal is your vocal inflection or tone. Put simply, if you are talking about something the prospect should be getting excited about, you need to sound excited yourself. You need to sound positive and happy from the moment you start the conversation. When you ask a question, you need your voice to sound inquisitive. Sounding bored or

---

11 For a more in-depth look at telephone sales and practice drills, visit www.sales-commando.com.

talking in a monotone is the quickest way to shorten a call and fail in your mission.

EXERCISE
Example of a basic script

This script will give you a foundation to work around when booking appointments.

The introduction and permission

You: 'Hi, is that John?'

Prospect: 'Yes.'

You: 'Good. This is Doug here from... We're a financial services company working in... The reason for the call is, very simply, you've been identified as someone who would benefit from our services, so what I would like to do is just take up two minutes of your time and tell you about how we add value to people like you, OK?'

67 WORDS, 22 SECONDS

The key to this ending is that your voice inflection assumes a positive response from the client. Start to raise your tone of voice when saying '... like you,' heightening it further when you say 'OK'.)

Prospect: 'Mmm, OK.'

The question and short story

You: 'Great, so before I begin and to make this call as quick as possible, may I just ask you a couple of questions?'

Prospect: 'Er, yeah.'

You: 'Thanks John. You obviously work. Are you self-employed or employed?'

Prospect: 'Employed.'

You: 'And how long have you been working with your current company?'

Prospect: 'Eight years.'

You: 'Did you come from another company, or have you been with the current company since the beginning?'

Prospect: 'No, I came from another company.'

You: 'And are you a family man, John?'

Prospect: 'Yeah.'

You: 'Okay. Well, it's good I called you today as we usually sit down with people when they've been working with your company for a few months. We basically help people organise their finances while they are on their journey, so they can make the most of the money they are earning. We deal with all manner of financial concerns from saving for your future to educating your kids, or making better use of that frozen pension you may have. There is a whole host of benefits and services. I suppose what I am saying is that if I could show you something that was perfect for you and saved you money, you would take a look at it, wouldn't you, John?'

Prospect: 'Well, yes.'

The close

You: 'Okay, that's fantastic. So, when is a good time to sit down with you? Morning, afternoon or evening?

I'm available on Tuesday at 10am, Wednesday at 12 or would you prefer Thursday at 2pm?'
254 WORDS, 1 MINUTE 48 SECONDS (BOOM)

Clearly, the basic script in the boxed example doesn't include any objections. However, what you need to concentrate on at all times is simplicity. This is a total of 254 words and your end of the air time should be no longer than 1 minute 45 seconds. Focus on the back end of the call – the positive outcome – and always try to get to third base, leaving out any unnecessary crap. Follow this method and I promise you, at the end of each day you will have scored a lot of points and as a result will have a lot of appointments too.

You may also like to refine your own script to ask more relevant questions depending on your country, territory and environment. This would also be shaped with any relevant information you may have gleaned about the prospect from the internet and other sources.

Face-to-face prospecting

Seminars

A seminar is a very versatile prospecting technique and can work well as a supplement to other prospecting methods. So, for example, if you can't quite make the sales appointment when you are prospecting at other events, or when you are cold calling, a seminar can be a good middle ground to reel the potential client in.

> **You:** 'I'm holding a seminar in a few weeks, David, where there will be loads more information about what we were discussing this morning. You'd probably find it really useful. I'll call you next week with all the details.'

It is a great hook to stay in contact and is the perfect way to pull a wavering prospect in.

The seminar itself can be something that you give in a workspace, or you can go the whole hog and rent a function room in a hotel. It can take many different shapes or forms. Indeed, you may not even call it a seminar at all. You could bill it as an 'information talk' and run it at a place of work that has lots of the type of people you are looking for all in one place. Ideally, if you have a choice, I would always advise getting your prospects away from their familiar environment to a completely separate venue where they are less likely to be distracted. However, if that doesn't work, any action with the right people is better than no action whatsoever. Find a location that works for you and give it all you've got.

The aim of the game with seminars is to invite anyone and everyone that fits into your demographic along. You will have to put a lot of effort into this process to get the right number of people there, not just send out a bunch of letters and hope for the best. This means being organised with your data and, again, there is some advice on this in the next chapter.

Be prepared that not everyone who says they will come along will turn up. Indeed, as much as 40 or 50 per cent might not show. You need to factor this in, plan the objective, give people a hook of interest and deliver it with passion and belief.

Don't be put off if the first seminar you hold doesn't work out and hardly anyone comes along. Keep going, because you will break the ice in the end and these events do gain traction over time, particularly if you give clients the value they seek. This was certainly the case with Will, one sales consultant I worked with who decided to take this particular approach. The first six seminars Will held were really not that great. In one case, only three people showed up. Good for Will, though – he persisted. Then, at seminar number seven everything changed. The bat was swung again and, boom: the sweet spot was hit and over 130 people attended. All were the perfect demographic too. Each person at Will's seminar was motivated to some degree and they all left their details, with most requesting a sit-down appointment with Will. He signed over forty new clients as a result of this action. Brilliant!

It takes organisation, effort and balls to run successful seminars, but they will definitely pay off when done correctly. Planning is the key to the door of success when holding any kind of event, small or large.

CASE STUDY
Presenting like a pro

The first time I was ever asked to make a presentation, I was really nervous about it. I'd been given two days' notice and told I had to present in front of about a thousand people. I only agreed to do it on the basis my company sent someone to teach me how to make a presentation properly.

I wrote out my presentation the night before meeting my presentation guru and learnt it off by heart like a ten-year-old. The next day, when I got in front of my teacher, he put a camera on me and said, 'Right, go.' I got about three lines into it and dried up completely. I forgot what I was saying after discovering at the worst possible moment it was impossible to memorise all the words in a half-hour speech.

The guru asked me what I was doing and I explained I had tried to memorise my speech but failed.

'Hold on a second,' he said. 'Can I ask you one question?'

'Sure,' I replied.

'This presentation you're giving – do you know more about the subject than anyone else in that room?'

'Yeah,' I nodded.

He looked at me long and hard and finally he said: 'Then that's the last and only thing you need to think about before you step out in front of them.'

That's exactly what I did and it went brilliantly. If you

know your stuff, you'll never fear anything.
Noel O'Leary, Executive Director

Social immersion

This plan of action requires exactly what the section title suggests, social immersion, but it is probably easiest to explain through the experience of one particular guy I coached who, in my opinion, perfected the technique. Let's call him Mark.

Firstly, Mark got complete buy-in from his entire family for his plan of action because it really did involve complete social immersion and quite a substantial upheaval for them all. To get started, Mark did his research to find an area where the majority of the demographic he wanted to connect with lived. Once the area had been pinpointed and thoroughly checked over, Mark found a house to rent smack bang in the middle of it.

Mark hired a professional company to get him and his family settled into their new home as quickly as possible, and within a few days they had the house looking immaculate. Mark then went door to door, explaining to his neighbours they were new to the area and asking them whether they would like to pop over that coming Sunday for a get-together.

'My family is really keen to get to know the neighbours,' he told them with a friendly, approachable smile.

The reaction in the neighbourhood was a pretty unanimous:

'Yeah of course, we would love to come,' they all said.

Mark was absolutely right in his assumption that, even if the neighbuors didn't particularly fancy going that weekend, they would be curious enough to overcome their lethargy because they'd want to check out the new guy. After all, who can resist a nose around a neighbour's house?

The barbecue was a huge success. The food was fantastic, the beer flowed and the music played. Everyone in the neighbourhood realised how much they enjoyed the opportunity to get together socially with people they usually only saw fleetingly as they rushed off to work. And who had brought them altogether? Mark, of course.

Mark didn't stop there. His aim was to meet and make friends with as many people as possible over the next few months and to make his the 'go to' house of the neighbourhood. He was systematic in this strategy, throwing regular barbecues, get-togethers and parties. If there was a big sports game on TV, Mark's family would be the ones hosting the viewing of it. If there was a game of golf happening, then rest assured Mark would be the one organising it.

It won't be a surprise to you to read that Mark and his family became very popular very quickly, and gained the friendship and trust of pretty much everyone in their now very close-knit area.

The next step in Mark's plan, to begin the process of reaping the fruits of his family's labour, was the easiest of all after the leg work they'd put in. In fact, it happened perfectly naturally. Gradually, without any prompting, people in the neighbourhood started asking Mark for advice.

'Hey Mark, you look after finances, don't you?' they'd say over a cool beer. 'We keep getting calls from some financial company we've never heard of and wondered what you thought of them.'

And so the avalanche began. Within an amazingly short space of time, most of the neighbourhood were taken on as clients and, of course, all became amazing advocates for Mark's services, freely recommending him to all their friends and family far and wide. Over a four-year period Mark has become a multi-millionaire.

Social immersion works. This approach is brilliant, it's totally dedicated and it absolutely gets results. Sure, it does take commitment and a certain degree of financial investment, but without a doubt it builds the deepest of foundations for the long game.

Formal client leverage

This final approach is another outstanding way of creating business, but this one does rely on you having a client book to start with.

Once again, it's easier to explain using a real-life example. When I first started mentoring Steve, he was clearly struggling with prospecting. Although he was making some money with his portfolio of around fifty-six clients, we both knew he was a long way from reaching his full potential when it came to prospecting. In fact, he was pretty discouraged by the whole thing, particularly because he felt he was constantly scratching around for appointments. Steve wasn't much of a social animal, so we were pretty sure the social immersion approach wouldn't work.

It seemed to me that Steve was a perfect candidate for the formal client leverage approach. We came up with a plan that centred on Steve committing to take, or offering to take, four existing clients out for a breakfast meeting twice per week.

The phone conversation in which he invited them went along the following lines.

'Hi, Steve here. Listen, I know we only met last month. However, I have selected a number of clients that I would like to take out to a business breakfast. It's obviously on me, but I would love you to come and there are a couple of other clients that I look after that I really want you to meet too. I think it will be beneficial for you to get to know them.'

Not everyone accepted initially, but we were prepared for that. Steve simply bowed out of the conversation by agreeing to keep the invite open and run it by them another time. Plus, in the early days, not everyone who agreed to come actually turned up. Indeed, on one particular breakfast literally no one came. However, to his credit, Steve persisted and kept organising and holding the meetings and clients gradually responded, sold in part on the opportunity to meet other like-minded business contacts. It also helped that the events themselves had a definite time period attached of between an hour and an hour and a half.

The breakfasts were laid-back affairs at a nice hotel near his clients' offices and Steve had a pre-rehearsed commentary on the current market planned should it be required if the conversation didn't flow. He also had a good, solid, third-party story of how another client had introduced him to this particular person or that to help him out with his finances, just to sow the seed of a referrals mindset among his breakfast guests. Plus, Steve always made sure he came along with a number of sealed envelopes detailing each individual's personal investment valuation to be handed to them at the end.

Steve's modus operandi was supremely subtle, though. He carefully cultivated a mindset that he was simply investing his time into his valuable clients, introducing them to one another and not pushing his own needs and desires down their throats. Nothing was asked for and no demands or requests – other than their company – were placed on the clients at all.

It took around two and a half months for Steve to actually achieve breakfast sittings with all fifty-six clients. Then, after this round, Steve then repeated the process and began to gain a far closer relationship with them. He then introduced the notion that, if they could think of someone else who would benefit from meeting with him, would they please let him know and he would accommodate them too. His clients obliged and pretty soon the breakfast club filled up with new faces.

Steve is now the most consistent and successful consultant I know and runs his breakfasts pretty much every day. That means that every single morning he starts his day with a brand new sales opportunity meeting another human being who understands what he does though powerful third-party endorsement. He is continuously growing his network and the cost to him is minimal too, because breakfast is an inexpensive meal.

This process took just six months to really start to yield results for this consultant. Steve was fully aware of this timeframe when we designed the plan of attack and, of course, he maintained other avenues of prospecting and doing business while his breakfast meetings built momentum.

If you think this approach may suit you, bear in mind it is not something you can rush. The strategy is about building deep, secure relationships with people, and that will take time. You could liken it to putting cement into the ground to build the foundations for a house. That cement of your relationship with your client has to be allowed to dry before you attempt to build on top of it. Then, once it is set, you can load it up and build that house higher and higher. You can benefit from the foundational relationship and start to leverage your position.

After a while, as you become established, it will get easier. You will gain momentum and when you meet with an introduction for the first time they will fully understand the way your breakfast club works. All being well, they'll arrive ready to provide you with other contacts in the form of referrals from the off. That is what you should be aiming for.

You'll know you've cracked it and your core foundation work is complete once 100 per cent of your sales pipeline starts to flow from this very secure place.

Maintaining the momentum

It may take some trial and error to find the prospecting strategy, or indeed combination of strategies, that works best for you. As I said above, you may even find a way to adapt a method to work better for your particular market. While you are going through this process and building your battle plans you must, of course, continue with your existing methods of prospecting. You would be foolish to stop everything else you are doing while you experiment with getting your new prospecting technique off the ground.

It will mean you've got to work a bit harder for a while, but if you've read this far I am assuming you are not a shirker. You can't afford to let your momentum slow down, even if it is part of a long-term plan.

If you are brand new to the business and just getting started, you simply need to hit the phone and wear out the shoe leather as well as everything else. Do anything and everything to gain traction as soon as possible. I would also give a serious amount of time to some of these more long-term strategies too. Eventually, the techniques here will take over and you will be glad you began the process, believe me.

If you've been doing this for a while, try out these new strategies concurrently with what you've always done. Then, once something takes off, you can ease off on less successful techniques.

Whatever happens, don't put it off. Start polishing and refining your prospecting process now. The sooner you start, the sooner you will be able to harvest the fruits of your labour and begin looking after all those new clients.

If you are hesitating, it can only be for one of three reasons:

1. You think it will take far too long.

2. You can't be bothered to put in this kind of effort.

3. You don't want to get too close to the clients.

Let's look at each of these excuses in more detail.

1. *It takes too long. Seriously?* Guys, listen: you are building a career here, one that will pay long-term dividends and financially provide you and your

family with ultimate security. If you want to get anywhere with this, you have to move away from the one-dimensional, cold approach that may currently be your number-one source of prospecting. If you don't you will never reach your optimum capacity and, even worse, you are likely to burn out chasing mediocre returns.

2. *It's too much effort.* If you can't be bothered or it seems like too much work, get out of the industry, now! Find something you can be bothered with. In fact, I'm not quite sure why you picked up this book.

3. *You don't want to get too close to clients.* Other than complete lethargy, this excuse gives me the greatest cause for concern. The only reason that I can imagine someone would be uncomfortable forming a relationship of total trust and transparency with a client is if they don't totally believe in what they are doing. Again, I will refer you to point two and ask you to seriously question whether you are in the right job.

Never lose sight of the fact that sales is the highest-paid hard work and lowest-paid easy work there is. If you are reluctant to pull your sleeves up and get stuck in, ask yourself: how much am I getting paid right now? If it is not an amount that inspires you, then what would inspire you?

Now you know how much you need to get your attention, you know what to do, don't you? Get out there and start taking prospecting seriously. Resolve to really go for it, be an entrepreneur and build your own economy with very solid foundations.

Procrastination is the thing that costs the dreamy sales professional the most money. Stop procrastinating and start doing.

Chapter four

GET ORGANISED

There is a bridge that needs to be constructed between sheer relentless activity and maximum productivity, and that bridge is called efficiency.

Basic survival techniques are an important part of Marine Commando training and I still vividly remember the way these potentially life-saving steps were drummed into me. Once again, this all took place in the less than hospitable environs of windswept Dartmoor in Devon, and this time my physical challenge was to learn the 'basic rule of three'.

At the core of this principle is the fact that the human body can, in general, last:

» three minutes without oxygen

» three days without water

» three weeks without food.

Clearly, in a combat scenario there are often many other factors that may affect your ability to stay alive, such as an enemy that's hell bent on killing you, or extreme cold that could freeze off parts you'd rather hang on to. However, those somewhat distracting factors notwithstanding, the fact is that in pretty much any scenario the three items listed above are the ones to which you should be paying the most attention. They *will* save your life. You need to attend to them in that chronological order too, because if you don't have the first the other two are no good, and if you don't have the first and second, food ain't going to help, and so on.

Like I say, I learnt the hard way how important these elements are, because, as you can imagine, the Royal Marines have a particular way of drumming a message home. I won't go into it in any detail here, because we're here to be sales commandos, not Marine Commandos, but I can attest that the learning I took away from the exercise was that, in a survival situation, you *must* get your priorities right.

You may well be wondering, 'How is this relevant to me?' After all, it is pretty unlikely that you'll be under imminent threat of suffocation or dehydration when you pop in to see a client about his pension fund (unless he *really* doesn't want to play ball, anyhow). Well team, the point of mentioning the rule here is to emphasise just how important it is for you to get your priorities right.

Being prepared and organised and covering all the bases in logical order are important parts of being elite. Your *oxygen* is derived from running your sales operation with military precision, with several databases all stuffed full of good, well-checked prospects. Holding regular meetings, seminars and events with a steady flow of suitable prospects is the *water* that sustains you and builds your business. Finally, the *food* that will nourish both you and your family is the growing portfolio of new clients you will service and look after with the utmost care. Neglect the basic rule of three at your peril. Each of these elements is essential to a successful sales operation and they come in that order of priority too.

Yet, over the years I have witnessed far too many sales professionals who've missed this point completely. They let themselves get distracted by the lure of big money without ever giving much thought to how they will go about earning it effectively. As a result, their priorities are all over the place and there is little or no organisation to how they tackle new business, look after their data or even care for existing clients. The result? They squander prospects' details, lose valuable pieces of information or make contact with extremely good prospects before they have done sufficient due diligence and research to properly communicate with them.

Examples of these poorly prioritised patterns are so prevalent that I'm going to highlight just a few more, just to ensure my point is crystal clear. They boil down to little more than diversionary tactics such as taking hours out of the day's prime selling time to do 'stuff' when you know you should be seeking new contacts, meeting new people, talking to potential customers and basically telling them all about what you do and how you do it. If you're not having a conversation with someone in some way about your services, or finding new people to have conversations with, you are not breathing. Or, to put it another way, if you are guilty of doing this you are killing off opportunities rather than creating them. You'll be wasting the vast majority of your hard work and ultimately you will suffocate your sales career because you'll be depriving it of its much-needed oxygen.

Of course, if you want to be hammering away at your sales funnel all the time, you've got to be on top of your paperwork. You need to know who you are talking to, who you've approached and what they said. You must have systems that are beyond reproach. Hunting around for lost contact information definitely falls into the category of pointless diversionary 'stuff'.

In short, if you want to be a sales commando, you've got to get organised.

Granted, the type of personality and character that generally moves into the sales profession is by nature not too enamoured with paperwork. Let's face it, we love selling, closing deals and meeting challenges head on. Our attitude is, 'Get me in front of people', not 'let's sit behind a desk shuffling paper.' That's what I'm like and I know you will be like that too.

If you want to be a sales commando, though, your systems need to be slick, fast, efficient and effective. You have to cover all the bases and address each part of the process, not just the bits you like. That means you've got to take care of the oxygen and water *as well* as the food. Sure, the best bit of the job is getting in front of someone and doing what you do best, but if you haven't covered all the bases at the back end you will be wasting your time because sooner or later you will run out of people to talk to. Just like my Marine Commando rule of three, these processes are all complementary. You can't have one without the other two.

If you are going to get in front of as many people as possible, you need to have a plan, with clearly defined priorities and a support structure that keeps you provided with opportunities. You also need to be super-organised to get the very most from each and every day. Never lose sight of the fact that, if you don't follow the basic rule-of-three process systematically, you will become forgetful and inefficient and will let people down. Similarly, whether you like structure, planning and paperwork or not, if you don't make time for plans, strategies and ultimate efficiency, you will be a busy fool (albeit a highly motivated one) who will be tring very hard and really not getting very far, or at least not as far as your efforts should be taking you. This scenario, my friends, would be enough to eventually sap the morale of any soldier and will almost certainly burn you out. If you don't want to let this happen to you, this chapter shows you what you have to do.

At the root of the sales commando organisational rule of three is a bank of well-maintained and highly efficient databases. These are your oxygen. This simple yet effective database system will contain several lists that will be run so effectively that nothing will pass you by. Your mission is to learn to capture leads and data in the right way, place them in the correct group and treat each record as the individual piece of precious information it is. The order of the day is to note down and manage as much data as possible and then use the intelligence gleaned from this information to communicate in a way that interests clients and makes them feel comfortable.

In the following sections I have outlined the range of databases you should be running. This system will help focus your mind and make you more productive, although, over time, you may like to adapt the scope of the databases a little to suit your own way of working.

First-attack power base!

This database will be your very first point of focus and is by *far* the most powerful one you will ever have. It's the list that is stuffed full of people with whom you are most closely aligned because they are your friends, family and close acquaintances. Team, the door is wide open to you with these guys and you've got tonnes of influence over them. Amazingly, though, considering this fantastic, glowing intro, this is the list that's just not used enough by sales professionals. Indeed, people tend to opt for cold calling over utilising this fantastic resource. Crazy.

To build your 'first-attack power base' (FAPB), write down the names of everyone and anyone you know: friends, family, team mates, everyone. Just list them out, noting down your relationship with them, their contact details and what they do for a living. Get down as much detail as you possibly can and be prepared to add to it as you go along.

Next, start calling them all up and building a little rapport, weaving some information about yourself into the conversation. Tell them what you are doing now and where you're working, and ask them whether they know anyone in your area or whether the company they work for deals with anyone in your field. Send them a friendly follow-up email reminding them of what you do.

Make time to take anyone on the FAPB whom you know quite well out for a coffee. The aim of the game here is to have a chat outside the environment where you usually see one another. This will be effective because it will help alert their subconscious to the fact something different is going on.

Maintain the personal touch and look after the connection that made you close in the first place. Think about doing things like getting to know the birthdays and anniversaries of everyone on this list and then giving them a call the week *before*. Everyone is bound to be sending messages on the day itself, but this way your communication will be memorable.

The objective of nurturing your FAPB is to employ the fantastic resource of people you already know to feed you with leads. The idea, though, is to sell *through* these people not necessarily *to* them. Do it right and they will pave the way for you to meet all sorts of valuable new prospects. While you're doing this you may even take some of your FAPB on as clients in the process.

Once you have combed your way through your list and a full understanding has been reached between you and the people on your FAPB, you can begin to activate and motivate them. In effect, you're trying to fully deputise, or recruit, them to bolster the ranks of people out there singing your praises, plus you want to get your hands on their contact books.

Don't be afraid to fully incentivise them either once you get them completely on board. Set out an official-looking agreement, or contract, between you that you can both sign. Make it clear that some form of remuneration will go their way whenever they find you a new client. Or, if you prefer, you could be slightly less formal and make up a colourful flyer listing the rewards they will receive if they introduce a certain number of new clients to you. For example:

» one new client: day spa treatment
» two new clients: dinner for two in a nice restaurant

» three new clients: electrical gadget of some kind
» four new clients: two-night stay in a hotel, or a short break away including travel costs
» five new clients: a bigger break, including an international flight.

Work out your average income per deal and commit a percentage to invest in your FAPB. Take great care your rewards list doesn't look cheap and nasty. Remember, it is much better to have 65 per cent of something than 100 per cent of nothing. You've got to make it worth their while or they will never buy into the process.

This type of incentive structure can be used in many ways across all of your marketing communications. Take it, model it and make it yours.

Team, I guarantee you that there is business in that FAPB list, lots of it, just waiting to be collected. It's right there in front of you; you just have to pick it up.

There are companies out there that totally subsist on their FAPBs: Nu Skin, Herbalife, Mary Kay, Amway and Avon all do, to name but a few. These are multi-billion-dollar companies that only exist thanks to the business they take from these databases.

If you run it well, your FAPB should be powerful, plentiful and productive. Make sure you reach for your FAPB file every single day to see what you can do to either add to it or cultivate it some more. You'll be amazed how much fruit it will bear.

The way I see it, I am like a personal trainer. Say you wanted to get a six pack, you could go down to the gym on your own every day, do tonnes of punishing crunches, eat healthily and so on. It's pretty easy to let yourself down, though. You'll turn to the snooze button instead of going to work out first thing, or you'll have that extra slice of cake. In all likelihood it is not going to happen to the extent you'd like it to.

If you have a personal trainer who meets you at the gym at six and frequently monitors your diet and progress, you'll be more likely to be committed to meeting your goals. You'll be up and at it because you won't want to let them down. Plus, their methods are effective because they'll tell you what weights to use, exercises to do and diet to eat.

It's exactly the same with finances. We all need our health and enough money to live a decent life. Left to themselves, most people will probably do nothing about their finances. That's where I come along.

Graham Bentley, Senior Area Manager

You-buy base

We are all customers of various companies and every single day we buy goods or services from all sorts of people. It stands to reason that, if they have you as a customer, they will have others just like you who are also their customers. It's the perfect demographic. All you need to do now is bridge that link.

The target with the 'you-buy base' (YBB) is to make contact with the companies you work with, talk to them and invest some time with them. Find out whether there is a way you can help one another.

An example of how this might work well would be if you lived and worked in an area where there was a high proportion of the correct demographic. It stands to reason that many other people who are just like you will be buying exactly the same products you buy from a small range of local suppliers. Imagine how powerful it would be to make contact with these other, like-minded, people in your neighbourhood through your common link, the local supplier. All you need to do is find a way to use the supplier you know as a point of focus, to gain momentum and place leverage. Call the owners and ask to meet them to discuss how you could add value to their business. Offer them the enticing prospect of working with you to improve the lot of their customers. Couch it in the right terms and they should see it as a positive advantage to working with you to give their customers this extra service.

The idea of this base, and indeed all the bases, is to create a focal point for your entrepreneurial ideas and skills. This base works particularly well in this respect. One example was performed with great ingenuity by a consultant I mentored in Spain. He wanted details of wealthy expatriates to approach, so he contacted water-delivery companies that serviced the housing areas that were the most likely dwellings for those expats. Together they worked on incentives to use the water company's data to invite customers to golf days and, pretty soon, he unleashed a rich stream of new clients.

This can be done in any country or town. It just takes inventive thinking and energy.

Another way to view this technique is that it is busting the rule of six degrees of separation. Six degrees of separation is the theory that everyone is six (or fewer) steps away from a connection with anyone else in the world. Thus, through the old friend of a friend system and thanks to technological breakthroughs in communication and travel, you could connect with absolutely anyone on the planet. Here, though, we're only trying to hop over just *one* degree of separation, by getting someone you already know to introduce you to someone they already know. What could be easier than that?

(As an aside, imagine how much business could be done if you could get all six degrees working for you. Maybe that is something we sales commandos should put on the list to tackle next year? Yeah, I think we'll do that.)

Try it now: the YBB is a little-used database but it can be hugely powerful. Plus, and here is the bonus, by going through this exercise you will be giving a new sense of focus to your mind. The very act of knuckling down and concentrating on the companies you work with and how they might offer some sort of leverage will open up all kinds of entrepreneurial thoughts. Who knows what this sort of activity might spur you on to do next?

Big-hitter list

The 'big-hitter list' is the one you use for your 'Big-Potential Clients' and I have to admit this is one of my personal favourites. This is your list of super-wealthy big-hitters, such as company CEOs, owners of large businesses and all-round really successful guys and girls. If you pull it off with these people, it will be *the* big deal or contract. Without a doubt.

Create a totally separate list for these targets and fill it with as many VIPs, business owners and wealthy people you can think of, or research and dig up, or (better still) that you actually know. Your target is to add detail to this list every single day. Find out where these people hang out, all the clubs where they are members, what their interests are and who is in their close circle of friends. Brainstorm how you're going to meet them and what steps you need to take to make that happen. Note down everything you can possibly think of, or find out, however insignificant it may seem, because sooner or later it may prove to be relevant.

Your ultimate aim is to transfer the people who feature on your big-hitter list to your FAPB. However, in the first instance, we will give them their own specific categorisation in your system to focus your attack and help you get into the correct mindset while you work out how to get their attention.

Another massive benefit of making a dedicated big-hitter list is that you will be able to get these big names off your mind when you are not refining your list. You won't waste hours daydreaming over what may happen with that big-potential client you've just met, discovered or talked to on the phone. It happens. I know it does and it is totally understandable. Just realise though, the more time you spend daydreaming, the fewer hours you'll be able to devote to other, no less essential, areas of your strategy. Give your big-hitters their own list and you'll rest easy knowing you're doing all you can.

I would also like to add a very big note of caution here. Don't allow yourself to get over-excited by this list and attempt to jump the gun in your enthusiasm. Prior preparation is everything. Moving too soon and trying to cold call a big-hitter to kick-start an introduction would be like trying to take on a tank with small arms fire. You may get extremely lucky (but the odds are massively not in your favour) but the more likely outcome is you will simply give away your position and get blasted into kingdom come.

These types of people are in high demand. They have gatekeepers protecting them from people like you and these gatekeepers are trained in the art of neutralising you and your efforts as soon as you call. They're ruthlessly effective too. You must take a different approach with these people. A true sales commando bides his time, gathers intelligence and will only strike when the chances of a favourable outcome are high.

A big-hitter list can prove to be hugely lucrative in the long term, but the only way it will be effective is if you tend to it every day. Every time you sit down at your desk, open up your big-hitter list and ask yourself what you can do to improve it today. What events should you be planning, or attending, that will attract the people that form part of this elite list of prospects? Give some thought as to how to meet them in the right way, at, say, the golf club, the health club or the gym. Think about the long game, gain their trust and then take things from there.

Having this big-hitter pool as a totally separate list is a winner. In my experience it is the core strategy of all the most successful consultants from around the world. It works for them, it worked for me and it will work for you, so use it.

Not-sold list
The 'not-sold list' will be quite substantial for many salespeople and is definitely the one that will grow the most rapidly. It's the nature of sales that you'll hear

'no' more than 'yes' and you can't allow yourself to get discouraged by this fact. As long as you are out there doing your stuff, you're going to get people constantly tagging on to this list. What is important is to keep a list of 'not solds' rather than just moving on, with never a backwards glance, as so many salespeople do. I have a theory as to why people shy away from keeping a list like this and it's down to two words: 'denial' and 'ego'.

That is crazy. You've already put in a great deal of effort, so don't give up at the first hurdle. Collate the details of your 'not solds' and put in place a concrete strategy to keep in touch.

If you still need some convincing, let's look at this list in terms of pure logic. To start with, let's make some assumptions. Let's say you've not been intentionally wasting your time with the people you've been targeting. You've obviously been striving to get in front of those that are from the correct demographic. Therefore, it would be safe to deduce that the vast majority of prospects you actually met yet didn't manage to close will fall into the 'should have, could have, would have, but didn't' category.

Therefore, if you continue in this train of thought, these leads have already effectively been through a net or filtering system of some kind, according to your own standards. This makes those 'not solds' a seriously valuable database. In fact, I often think, if you could get hold of the 'not-sold' list of a competitor, be it a different company or perhaps a competitive work colleague, that would be pretty damn lucrative. But let's stay out of trouble for now and stick to our own 'not solds'. My hope is, by now, you can see the logic of maintaining a connection with the ones who got away.

Don't waste too much time wondering why they said no. There are so many reasons as to why a particular person does, or doesn't, decide positively when you first speak. Most of the time, the prospect won't even be able to articulate why they said no. The fact they didn't commit before could even be because you didn't present yourself to them in the *exactly* correct way on that day. Or maybe you just didn't connect in a way that was in tune for them and their mood *at that time*. Remember though, they are, at some stage, going to be a client of someone, somewhere. They will, in the end, do something with someone, be it their local bank, an internet-based financial service, another brokerage or even perhaps another consultant in your brokerage. But, if they are going to do business with someone, that someone should, most definitely, 100 per cent, without a doubt, be you. It's your job as a sales professional to take them the rest of the way. It is up to you to hold their hand and lead them through the journey to the close. You've got to turn that no into a yes.

Don't allow yourself to squander these individuals. A sales commando shouldn't lose any fish from the net. We want to land them all, one after another.

The first thing to do when dealing with 'not solds' is to ensure you accurately record all their details and don't lose them. Then, you need to give some serious thought as to how to re-approach them more intelligently, so, when they do eventually travel the last few yards to their 100 per cent buying decision, they buy from, and commit, to you.

Bear in mind you will need an entirely new strategy. The adage that always comes to mind here is: when you re-approach, take a different approach. It doesn't exactly take a genius to work out that using exactly the same method when trying to close a previously failed prospect is probably going to turn out quite badly.

Instead, work on ways to build a relationship with your 'not solds'. This is the list that should be getting the invites to your open days, networking events, business breakfasts and seminars. Think of imaginative ways to stay in touch with 'not solds' and make sure they perceive these ideas as useful to them as individuals, rather than simply being a way for you to hound them towards making that sale.

The worst possible way to go about this would be to call every now and again to say something like, 'Hi, have you thought any more about that savings plan?'

The prospect will automatically think, 'Well, no I haven't because I still don't want one, thanks.'

You need a strategy and a totally different, innovative approach to keep these people interested and ensure they don't swim into another person's net. Work at building their trust so they become your customer and not someone else's.

> I was up against another guy, who made a pretty good job of slagging off the company I worked for, so I didn't get the business. I stayed in touch with the client though and, sure enough, two years later, he was back.
>
> 'I've come back to you because the impression you made on me back when we first met and then since is much better than the guy I've been doing business with,' he said when he telephoned.
>
> I saw him again and signed him up on the spot. Plus he gave me five referrals without me even pushing for them.
>
> *Chris Withers, Area Manager*

Cold base

The final list is the uninvitingly named 'cold list'. This is, of course, the cold, freezing data you obtain in one form or another as you go along. Compared to the other databases, each name on this list shouts 'hard work'. None of this is to say this is some sort of rubbish bin of a list; it is simply that you must tell yourself that cracking all, or even part, of this list is going to take some supreme dedication on your part. If you want to turn this non-efficient data into gold, you will have to motivate yourself to be totally up for it, engage yourself completely with it and hammer away as hard as you can.

Oddly, in my experience, salespeople often use this base the most regularly even though it's obviously the most unproductive. Cold calling is part of the job, I totally get that, but it should never be the *only* part of the job, or even the dominant part. Actually it should never be a majority shareholder of your time; it should only ever be a minority one.

I suspect the reason why this base is so frequently leaned upon is because servicing the other databases efficiently requires maximum effort and ingenuity. Looking after big-hitters, or the people on your FAPB list, for example, often requires lateral, out-of-the-box thinking, as well as time, energy and occasionally some financial investment too. The alternative of trudging through cold data can be a less challenging use of your time and, in addition, you'll be able to kid yourself you are doing absolutely everything you can to gain maximum traction and are working hard. Of course, the opposite is true and, without a firm plan of action, most of the time you do invest in your list will be wasted anyway.

My advice to you would be to be efficient, selective

and thorough with your cold data but not to fall into the trap of making it your main focus. Attack it for a maximum of forty-five minutes to an hour every day and you will find it bears fruit. Begin with an attitude and plan like this and you will find your cold list adds value to your life instead of eroding your morale and ruining your territory by getting you and your company a negative reputation.

As with all your databases, be as organised as you possibly can. Be ruthless with the names you add to it and never settle for mediocrity or poor-quality opportunities. This means that, when you add to your cold list, you must thoroughly research every name that you enter onto it because, team, if you pitch to crap you're gonna get crap. Over the years I have witnessed hundreds of sales professionals burning valuable time every day on prospects that would never bear fruit in a million years. It is soul destroying because they usually work so hard at it. I'll listen to them exercising incredible verbal skills on the phone, using some great positive techniques, but ultimately it was a complete waste of energy. Yes, they usually get *some* results. The problem is, the results they gain are disproportionate to the sheer effort and skill levels they are demonstrating. The end result to this unbalanced, misguided form of action is simple: eventually deep-seated negativity and dissatisfaction spill over into every other part of their work, affecting everything. A salesperson who constantly has to battle this hard for scraps of business will quickly burn out.

Please, please, please: only add data to your cold base that is suitable for you to call. Do your level best to assess the correct demographic of each prospect and judge whether they could have a positive effect on your pipeline.

As a bonus, when you get organised, it is highly likely you will come across people who should be added to your big-hitter list, YBB or FAPB while you are going through your cold list drills. That is great because it means you will be well on the path towards categorising these people in the most effective way. It will ensure you'll take a different approach next time you speak to them. That, in turn, means you'll be more in tune with what they need, which will help you create more successes for yourself.

Punch out a good-quality forty-five minutes or hour every day on your cold list and you will find it to be a very productive weapon in your arsenal. Get yourself into the right mental state and attack it.

The system

Where focus goes, energy flows. [12]

A system is a set of interacting or interdependent components forming an integrated whole.

---

12   Tony Robbins, American life coach (1960–).

How you set up your databases is totally up to you. Many people favour electronic files that can be categorised as a dedicated software system, or you may prefer the old-fashioned approach of keeping your various databases in differently coloured lever-arch folders. Personally, I prefer the second approach because I like to have my databases right there in front of me on the desk. They act as a constant physical reminder and, if I ever have a spare five minutes or so, I reach out for one and think, 'What can I do to improve this database?' Or, 'How can I find three new names for my big-hitter list?' Or, 'Let's approach half a dozen "not solds" and invite them to breakfast.' It's all a question of taking some massive action to generate some massive activity.

Setting up and maintaining the database system outlined in this chapter will cultivate a lucrative stream of incredibly warm prospects for you. It's a hugely efficient use of your time, too. The added bonus is, you will never be left with that feeling that you'd like to be doing something but don't really have a clue where to start. Your fantastic database will provide you with a constant flow of tasks to fulfil. In fact, I defy you to ever be bored at work again.

Far too many sales are lost because people don't get organised or follow up leads when they should. This database system is guaranteed to boost your productivity and get results. So, get prepared, be organised and remember the three principles of oxygen, food and water that will ensure you don't just survive in sales, you thrive.

Getting organised is not a desire. It's an absolute necessity. Focused efforts create productivity.

Chapter five

HANDLING OBJECTIONS

Nothing happens to me, it happens because of me.

Objections are a part of life. They happen all the time, every day, both inside and outside the sales arena. Face up to the fact they are going to happen to you and happen a lot. It's the way you deal with them, though, that makes all the difference between becoming a million-dollar financial adviser and one who makes an average, or slightly below-average, income.

Sales professionals are generally their own worst enemies when it comes to objection-handling. All too frequently they give undue weight and gravitas to the smallest murmurs of dissent. Over the years, I have witnessed all manner of unbelievably stupid, knee-jerk reactions and botched, nerve-wracked explanations to what started off as a fairly simple statement, or opinion, from a prospect. I have sat in meetings watching mountains being created out of molehills, which only serves to drive prospects further and further from a happy conclusion.

The advisers who react in this out-of-proportion manner are always so swept up in the process of striving for a signed sale in *absolutely every* meeting that they will regularly talk themselves out of a deal. In their over-eagerness, they fail to listen to what the prospect is actually trying to say. It's over-selling, pure and simple.

The upshot of this behaviour is always the same: something that could have been dealt with very simply and swiftly becomes a huge problem. Ultimately the only possible outcome is that the adviser's over-reaction becomes a deal stopper.

The crazy thing is, most objections are not objections at all, not at the beginning anyway. They are simply small reservations, or gripes, or little comment-like moans. They may just show nervousness to commit on behalf of the prospect. These objections should be listened to, smiled at and brushed aside. (There is more information on the reasons behind objections in the next chapter, where I will outline some advanced objection-handling techniques.)

There is another, very positive, way of looking at it too. If a prospect has decided to vocalise their concerns, it means they are giving you a chance to answer them. It is a definite interest indicator. If they were totally disinterested, they'd be trying to keep the meeting as short as possible, leaving no room for you to jump in and deal with the concern positively.

Whatever the reason for the objection, though, a sales commando should remain positive at all times and never, ever, fall apart at the first sign of things not going to plan.

I've found a great way to help keep things in proportion when a prospect starts saying they are not sure about something. Create a mental picture of each objection as a small monster being born and figuratively popping out of the prospect's mouth. The minute you pay attention to the fledgling monster you will be feeding it with energy, because this little monster thrives on encouragement. The more you acknowledge its presence, the more it will grow and grow. If you start flapping around and throwing out all sorts of ill-thought-through rebuttals, this objection monster will become very large, very fast indeed. A large, angry beast is, of course, something no sales commando wants on their hands, so it stands to reason the objection monster needs to be terminated quickly and efficiently.

The fastest and most effective way to dispatch an objection monster is to simply acknowledge its existence and then dismiss it, or quickly deal with it, depending on its source. You are effectively stopping it in its tracks before it has a chance to grow.

At this early stage, it is just a tiny objection monster, no more significant than an amoeba. React properly and it can be squashed and forgotten. If you spend too long on the job, going over and over why it doesn't deserve to exist, then it will gain power and energy from your attention. Pay too much attention to anything in your life and it will develop and grow to monstrous proportions (well, within reason; calm down guys). Once an objection monster gets to a certain size it will be almost impossible to defeat. So, whatever you do, *don't feed the beast*!

This doesn't mean you should ignore objections altogether, either. It is absolutely essential you uncover them, flush them out and properly deal with them, otherwise you will lose the trust and commitment of your prospect.

If you are on board with the assertion that once the objection monster has been born it must be dispatched, it's time to look at some powerful kill-the-beast manoeuvres, or objection-handling techniques. What follows here is an easy-to-follow three-stage process that should see even the most ugly objection monsters off at the pass.

Skyfall

The oldest and strongest emotion of mankind is fear and the oldest and strongest kind of fear is fear of the unknown.[13]

Since leaving the Marines I have sought out hobbies and pastimes that challenge me and give me that much-needed adrenaline rush through my veins. One pursuit

---

13   H.P. Lovecraft, author (1890–1937).

that I have taken up and stuck with is skydiving. I think the reason I like it so much is that it is one of the very few things you can do where you instantly become completely focused and totally and utterly consumed in the moment. When you jump out of that plane, nothing – but nothing – else whatsoever is on your mind.

I mention this thrilling hobby now because, when I go skydiving, I regularly witness objections and objection-handling in its most graphic and raw form. The place I skydive caters for both individual skydivers and people looking for a one-time, fun experience called a tandem jump. These tandem jumpers are strapped to an instructor, or tandem master as they are known.

Generally, it all begins nicely enough. While on terra firma, there are a lot of smiles and much nervous anticipation about the experience ahead. Then, after we board the plane and begin to gain altitude, expressions begin to change as the severity of the situation begins to fill everyone's minds. This is the moment you see people begin to check and re-check equipment. By the time the plane begins its jump run and the door on the side of the fuselage is opened, filling the plane with cold air, things change still further. Nervous jumpers see others shuffle to the doorway to begin exiting the plane one by one, and this is when a lot of tandem customers begin to have an 'objection moment', some extremely vocally indeed.

The way the tandem master handles the wobble goes

something like this: 'Yes, I know, it's scary. Don't worry, you're gonna love it. Now, head back, arms folded, here we go.' Then, boom, before the panicking jumper can grab the side of the exit hole on the aircraft and threaten litigation, they are out, falling through the air at 120 miles per hour, screaming at the top of their lungs. Of course, their screams very quickly change to utter euphoria as the sheer beauty of the experience consumes them and they are at one with life. They are in dazzling free fall. They smile, enjoy and don't want it to end.

In my view, this tandem master handles the objections in exactly the right way. He is full of confidence, listening to what the customers have to say, agreeing at first, then simply brushing it aside and doing what he knows the customer really wants and needs. Of course, the tandem master is also a true professional, in control and completely confident in his ability. He knows how to observe the client properly and recognise what is just a standard objection and what is something far more serious that requires a totally different approach.

I often imagine what would happen if I put some of the financial services professionals I work with in the tandem master's place. I reckon it would play out something like this. The salesperson would look at the fear in the client's eyes and mirror it. He'd probably then get into a long discussion, or even argument, about what was actually going to happen. After that he'd re-describe all the procedures to the poor panicking jumper. After failing to assuage their fears, he would pull the door of the fuselage shut and shout to the pilot to re-land the plane. After landing and taking off all the gear, the salesperson would walk the potential client into the office and re-explain the whole situation to them once again. This poor financial-services-run parachute school would go out of business within weeks!

I bet if you carried out an in-depth time-and-motion study of the number of times this situation actually happens across the entire financial service industry, you'd get a surprise. The scenario where a financial adviser meets a prospect and incorrectly deals with an objection happens far more than you'd ever imagine. If you then went on to calculate just how much money is lost because of this dithering across the industry in any one day, let alone a year, the figure would be frightening. If you don't believe me, carry out this exercise for yourself. Think about all the meetings you have been at over the past twelve months and picture the moments that you got totally caught up in some kind of debate about a minor point. Somehow you allowed yourself to become totally focused on the micro instead of the macro and then completely over-egged the cake in response. Add up all the possible opportunities that have been lost because of this wasted time (and follow-on business as a result). For many salespeople, it will be a terrifying number. This exercise can only be done by the consultant whose head isn't full of his own bullshit, because it takes a strong person to see it as it is. So, be honest and acknowledge your shortcomings and strive for improvement. Are you strong? sales commandos are.

Find their driver before they drive away

When we enter into a sales environment it is our job to uncover what buttons to push to get the prospect moving in the right direction. These buttons are called the client's 'drivers'. Everyone has them, even though most people don't know what their own ones are, probably because they haven't thought about the matter very much or because they've never had them pointed out to them properly. However, you would be surprised at how quickly it is possible to expose one or two of these drivers very early on in a conversation.

> I look for a natural moment to close off rapport and then I say, 'Okay, brilliant, let's get down to business.' Then, at that moment, I pull out a pre-typed agenda. It will have the date and name of the person on the top and there will be two copies, one for them and one for me. I hand them their copy and begin to read mine out loud, to help them be fully aware of the process that they are about to take part in. It lists:
> 1. introduction to the company

2. finding out what they have got
3. finding out what they want to achieve
4. discussion of issues arising from the above
5. agreement to the next steps.

Then, having gone through the agenda, I swap control. I spin my agenda around to face them and ask them a question: 'Is there anything that you want to add to today's meeting?'

After asking this question with a smile, I am still shocked and surprised by the number of people who say, 'Yeah, you know what, I have this personal pension that has been on my mind and some concerns over inheritance tax planning too...'

Then all I do is note down exactly what they've said next to number four on the agenda, saying: 'Okay, thanks for that. I'll ask questions specifically about those points when we go through them and I will treat them as a priority for you.'

Andrew Oliver, Senior Area Manager

During the course of your initial consultation, you should constantly be looking for as many drivers as possible because these will prove invaluable should objections arise later. These drivers are usually gaps in the way the client is organising his or her financial life.

It is worth bearing in mind there are only two motivators in life: the pursuit of pleasure and the avoidance of pain. Both are powerful influencers and each has its time and place; however, the stronger motivator by far is the avoidance of pain. It's that survival mechanism that kicks in and forces you to instantly act and find a way out. The avoidance of pain is the driver you are most looking for if you want instantaneous and rapid movement from a prospect.

I have watched thousands of consultants attempt to master this driver; however, very few (yep, probably 20 per cent) really ever execute this part perfectly. When dealing with pain as a motivator it is important not to become perceived as the perpetrator. While it's important to uncover pain in a client's portfolio, you need the prospect to feel you looking at it together. It is rather like a surveyor inspecting a home and pointing out a worrying structural defect that simply must be fixed. In an ideal scenario, the client would turn to you and say something like, 'Let's get that fixed ASAP,' or, 'How can we fix it?' You will need to practice to get the balance right.

Finding the prospect's driver is key, even if it may not be the actual basis on which you eventually end up doing business. Finding it will get them moving in the first place and that's an extremely powerful action in the sales process. It instantly removes any resistance to change on behalf of the prospect and, once you've done that, you've done 60 per cent of the job.

Be very inquisitive regarding the prospect's possible motivators and you won't go far wrong. Indeed, if you do it well, you will increase your chances of securing the business dramatically.

I sat down with one client who had been unhappy about his last experience with a financial adviser.

I said, 'Okay, did you feel like you learnt anything from the other guy?'

'No,' said the client. 'He was just trying to sell to me.'

'But you didn't buy from him?' I prompted.

'No, there was no point, he was only interested in selling a product,' insisted the client.

After that I spent a lot of time reassuring him that I was fundamentally different in the way I worked and that my job was to provide him, the client, with enough knowledge so he could make an informed decision himself. He liked the fact he was buying my technical expertise and that he perceived he had some control. He stayed with me.

Chris Withers, Area Manager

Let's look at some set-piece plays to see off objections.

Some set-piece plays
Phase 1: The brush-off
That's right: simply brush off the objection.

> **Prospect:** 'I don't really like the thought of a structured regular savings plan.'
>
> **You:** 'Yeah, I agree, lots of people say that kind of thing. It's just a fact of life that we all have to use them to build some sort of meaningful savings.'

31 WORDS, 11 SECONDS

Now you've swatted the monster, you must confirm you've made a clean kill and it is completely dead. Don't make a huge deal out it. All you need to do for this is a little body-language confirmation. Make eye contact, give your prospect a little smile and a shrug. Watch carefully for some kind of mirroring from him or her. If the prospect responds and you see their assent, then boom, you have your first confirmed kill. You are good to go and ready to move forwards with the sale.

The wrong approach in this instance would go something like this:

> **Prospect:** 'I don't really like the thought of a structured regular savings plan.'
>
> **You** (speaking quickly and forcefully): 'But, why not? Why do you feel that way? It's an amazing product and it has been hugely successful. Let me just list all the benefits…'

And off you go, bamboozling the poor prospect with every feature and benefit under the sun, blithely ignoring the fact their arms are firmly crossed at their chest and their eyes have glazed over. In my mind's eye, when I see this happening, I always wonder whether an Alien-like objection monster is going to burst out of their chest when they uncross their arms as they get up to rapidly exit the unproductive meeting. If your approach is like this, you are feeding that beast. Stop it.

This is not to ignore the fact that positive, open, investigative questions are an important part of good selling because obviously they are. However, everything has a time and a place and in these initial discussions this is not the right time.

Constructing a sale is like constructing a sentence. You must learn and master the language and rhythm of sales to give it meaning. Then it will allow you to travel to places you have only ever dreamed about.

You've got to learn to pitch it right when you are dealing with half a million of a client's money. Sometimes that means you have to back off completely, or other times you just defuse the situation. The important thing is not to anger them, because that gets them on the back foot and it's really difficult to go anywhere after that. My approach is to explain that what I am saying makes sense and is the right thing to do for them. I'm very specific too. Then I leave it up to them. Most people respond to that.

Aggressiveness is not going to help.'

Andrew Lockyer, Senior Consultant

Phase 2: Cuffing

One of the first lessons you learn in the early stages of Marine basic training is to pay complete attention to detail, in everything, at all times. You begin by learning how it applies to the simplest of things such as washing and shaving and then the training grows and evolves to cover everything, including looking after your weapon correctly. The training begins by showing recruits the right way to do things. You are then given a chance to practice the right way, and then you are expected to do things the right way from there on in. Every action is thought through, practised thoroughly and regularly inspected.

Recruits are told that one small error is, in itself, an action taken, because they have clearly consciously chosen not to do something right. And that, my friends, creates a reaction that could be, to the layman, perceived as somewhat extreme!

I once left my locker open. A marine's locker contains

all of their possessions, including every piece of clothing and equipment they have. This locker takes up part of a marine's bed space, not that much time is permitted for the luxury of sleep. Every morning, for the first ten weeks of basic training, a marine will stand by his bed while a full locker inspection is undertaken. The contents of the locker has to be placed in a certain order and pattern, with all clothing folded into an A4-sized bundle, matching the dimensions of the *Globe and Laurel* magazine, which is the Royal Marine Corps' monthly news magazine. If anything is out of place, the culprit is severely punished.

One morning, following such an inspection, I threw my weapon into my locker in a rush, because the corporal was screaming at us to run outside and fall in with the troop. As I turned to dash out I snapped the padlock on the locker door, locking it tight shut. Or, so I thought.

The corporal came outside with a big smile on his face.

'Tucker, you have made my day,' he shouted at the top of his lungs. 'Do you know what you have done?'

I was utterly confused. In my heart of hearts, I wanted to believe that I had done something good and was about to get commended; however, the corporal's tone and the impending feeling of doom were telling my subconscious that this was almost certainly not the case. Unfortunately, my subconscious was right.

'You left your fucking locker open!' boomed the

corporal, in full voice. 'Now get in there and empty the entire contents into your seaman's kit bag and bring it outside. You have ninety seconds and your troop awaits you. *Go!'*

Every recruit is issued a seaman's kit bag. It's a big brown canvas bag and it is just about possible to compress everything you own inside it with a lot of squeezing.

I ran inside, extremely conscious that I didn't want to make the whole troop late because this would begin a chain of punishment I really did not want to contemplate. I stuffed my entire life into the kit bag, heaved it up onto my shoulder and ran outside to re-join the waiting troop. I then had to carry it around on my shoulder, not just that day but for ten days after that. I carried that bag everywhere we went: into the lecture room, to the parade ground, to the gym, to the heads (the toilet), everywhere. Not only was this a serious pain in the arse and exhausting but also the admin nightmare it brought me every evening was extreme. At the end of each day everything had to be emptied out, re-ironed, folded and placed back in the locker ready for inspection the next morning. Then, the next day, it had to be promptly shoved back in the sack to be humped about all day again.

One tiny action created a reaction that was torture. Funnily enough, I never left my locker open again. Lesson learnt.

Fortunately, extreme reactions like this are rare.

However, everything you do in life and sales has some kind of outcome. Pay attention to detail and you will start to get your desired outcomes. Neglect the details and the outcomes will start to manage you, and not in a good way.

Remember: every action creates a reaction, no matter how small. Sometimes a small action from a financial consultant can result in them having to hump a load of failed and negative opportunities around on their shoulder for weeks. Don't let it happen to you.

This brings me to the second phase of the assault on objections, which is very simple and needs to be delivered quickly and casually. It is an action that should follow Phase 1 immediately if you sense, in any way, that the first phase wasn't totally successful and the little blighter is not dead.

Before we go into it in detail though, I'd like to throw in a few important caveats. The first thing to remember is not to panic, or you'll be right back to where you started. When dealing with objections you must always address them in a way that says there really isn't a problem and any small hiccup will be sorted out one way or another. Your priority is to put your prospect's mind at rest, make them comfortable, guide them and, if at all possible, make working with you a somewhat enjoyable experience. Don't, whatever you do, fall into the trap of introducing any unnecessary stress into your conversation, just because you haven't immediately succeeded in seeing off a challenge or objection. The more you stammer and leap about when things don't immediately go your way, the worse the situation will become and the bigger the objection monster will grow.

You also need to be mindful that, at the early stages of your relationship with the prospect, before it is properly evolved, you must be constantly aware of the delicate nature of the rapport. This is not to say there won't be a need for you to be strong at some point, when needed. It is simply to urge you to never, ever attempt to use unnecessary force to see off the objection monster. Right now, gently does it.

If you are happy with all that, let's proceed to the second phase. The action you need to turn to is called 'cuffing'. Don't try to read too much into the term; it's just an analogy for effectively acknowledging the objection and placing it in check to deal with at a later date. You are effectively taking the objection monster prisoner while it is still stunned, before coming back to it later.

It should go something like this: 'Okay, I can see you're not convinced. [pause] 'Let's just park this to one side and come back to it later when we need to discuss ways of meeting certain targets, shall we?'

Then, make a note of the issue on your pad and make a point of fully acknowledging that you've recorded it by showing the note to the client. Then, move on with your meeting. You must, of course, deal with the issue at some stage. In my experience, though, if this particular scenario has been played out correctly by the time the salesperson goes back to the objection, the client is often happy enough by this stage to kill it off themselves. Thanks to all the subsequent work you've done since they first raised the objection, they'll now fully understand the implications of their financial circumstances. However, don't get complacent. You must always return to the objection to gain this affirmation.

Phase 3: Full battle
Okay, so the final approach is the one you use when the objection monster seems immune to all other forms of reason and seems determined to take over. You've clearly got a battle on your hands in which you'll have to defeat this interloper, but at the same time you need to pull off the balancing act of not feeding the beast by giving it too much of your energy. If you get the balance wrong, you will unleash the monster completely and it will wreak havoc on your sale.

Before you embark on a full battle plan, with the aim of killing the monster stone dead, you must begin by identifying exactly what kind of monster it is that you are dealing with and how big it has grown.

Start by saying something like, 'Okay, so I can see this is still a concern for you. Let's work through this together. May I ask, what is the biggest single thing that bothers you about regular savings plans? And, on a score of one to ten, where would you place the level of that concern?'

51 WORDS, 19 SECONDS (KAPOW!)

In the worst-case scenario, you might get an answer like this:'Well, I want instant access to 100 per cent of my money at all times and I don't want anyone or anything telling me I can't touch my money. Therefore, the level of concern for this is nine out of ten. To be honest, I feel completely trapped when I think of getting tied into some kind of contract for a long period of time.'

I think we can all agree that this response shows there is already a pretty large monster in the room and you have quite a tough fight on your hands. In for a penny, in for a pound, though; you can't stop now. sales commandos never give up, remember?

Take the opportunity offered by the prospect's candid admission to press them further. In fact, try to get all their objections out in the open by questioning them on the next objection and the next. After all, if you are going to go into full attack mode, you'd be wise to gain all the intelligence you can before you make any rash moves.

What you need to do now is find a strategy to defeat the monster.

The first step in the fight is to repeat back to the prospect the things they have outlined. The psychology behind this is to demonstrate that you are clearly listening to their concerns and it allows them to hear what their words actually sound like.

> **You:** 'If I understand this correctly, you want some level of financial security for the future, but you are very nervous of tying up any of your cash in a regular saving plan? You'd like to dip into your funds as and when you feel the need, even though you are fully aware this could substantially erode the cash pot?'

Often with the correct use of voice inflection and tone, effectively emphasising or over-dramatising the right words, you can make the entire objection seem a little bit silly. This is a useful technique to soften up the objection monster, before steaming into it. Indeed, when delivered perfectly, sometimes this technique alone is enough to kill it. The prospect will hear you vocalise their doubts, realise they sound a little ridiculous and distance themselves from them. You may even hear them say something like:

> **Prospect:** 'Actually, now that you have said it back to me in this way, it does sound a little silly.'

Boom, you are almost there. The objection monster is gasping for its last breaths. Don't start celebrating just yet though. You still need to strike the *coup de grâce*, the killer blow to affirm that it is indeed dead. Finish the job like this:

> **You:** 'So you are happy to proceed and are open to exploring more about the subject of savings plans? If it helps, why don't you think of it this way: if you were me and you knew that the use of a particular product would cure a problem for a client, you would be keen to recommend it, wouldn't you?'
>
> **Prospect:** 'Yes.'

You: 'Excellent.'

Job done. Congratulations, you supreme slayer of objection monsters.

Just to take this one stage further though, let's do one further exercise in Phase 3. Let's assume you've come up against an objection monster that is fully equipped with Kevlar body armour and an invisible force field, so your first attack didn't work. You will now need a new, more powerful, plan of attack. So let's up the ante on your counter-assault.

To do this, we need to flip back to the first full battle attack, to the part where you made the repeat back. To recap:

> **You:** 'If I understand this correctly, you want some level of financial security for the future, but you are very nervous of tying up any of your cash in a regular saving plan? You'd like to dip into your funds as and when you feel the need, even though you are fully aware this could substantially erode the cash pot?'

Now, imagine that, instead of capitulating, the prospect is resolute in keeping the objection alive. They give an answer like:

> **Prospect:** 'Yes, that's correct.'

To crush this objection monster, we need to enter into the field of categorisation selling. If you are unfamiliar with the term, categorisation selling is a technique that makes choices easier to make. The secret to doing this well is to lay out a series of small steps that are going to lead the client inexorably towards making the decisions you desire.

It may help here to explain a little more about categorisation selling, which is something I've picked up from some truly talented professionals who seem to naturally slip into this mode when they are persuading somebody to make decisions or move forwards. All I have done is refined the technique, codified it and given it a name.

Ultimately, when we are selling we are always trying to get someone to make choices.

To begin this categorisation technique, we need to place prospects who have concerns, questions or objections into two very broad categories:

1. They are not sufficiently motivated to take action or make the next step.

2. They don't fully understand what you are proposing.

The reason for doing this is to understand which category the prospect sits in, so you can then clearly set out a series of small steps that will effectively reduce the problem bit by bit by helping the prospect make the right choices.

As sales professionals, we all naturally categorise to a certain extent. However, the very best ones lay an easy-to-follow path that leads people very smoothly and naturally in the direction they wish them to travel.

In the above instance, for example, you can set out a series of choices around a particular solution or product if you can see the prospect belongs in category two and doesn't understand what you are selling. Alternatively, if they fall into category one and are simply not sufficiently motivated, you can work at helping the prospect to see the gaps they may have in their financial life.

It is important to get the priorities right on the categories. Don't, for example, fall into the trap of categorising in huge detail, drilling down into everything, such as the type of investment fund that may be used to help achieve growth on a client's money. The art of categorisation is to steer them towards more general choices, agree those first and then get down to the nitty gritty.

For example, if you are thinking in terms of categorisation, a quick exchange in the very early stages of a meeting should go something like this:

> **Prospect:** 'So, tell me how to invest my money.'
>
> **You:** 'Well, I can absolutely cover that. However, let's just zoom out for a second and look at some other things first. For example: is it right for you to invest right now? If so, within what kind of structure? Then, what style and blend of investment would suit you?
>
> 'You see Mr Client there are a number of very important choices to make long before we get into that kind of detail. However, I love the enthusiasm.'

If you are not careful, it's easy to fall into the sales trap of being too specific too quickly. It happens all the time. Even the best of us can be rapidly drawn into a micro view and end up getting stuck, locked out or objected against, all because we have been unwittingly drawn into concentrating on minor differentials on a given subject when we should have been attempting to agree on far more simple and general terms. Remember, getting people to make choices, decide and agree on things throughout the *whole* sales process is incredibly powerful.

Indeed, the reason this categorisation technique is so effective is because it relies on the power of choice. Although we all make choices all the time, the real psychological value relies on our ability to perceive differences between the options. Thus, when we are shopping for something and want to make decisions, we want it to be easy. To complete the process quickly, we need to speedily identify what aisle to walk down or area of the store to visit. However, we also need to perceive that when we are in that area we are making our own very clear decisions about what we are actually going to buy. The fact that all the choices are effectively being made for us is camouflaged by the clever way the store has categorised and displayed the products.

Supermarkets are a great example in this respect because they are choice-making machines. When you enter one of these places the whole buying experience has been laid out to ensure that making choices, and therefore the purchase, is simple and easy. When anything is an easy experience it is inevitably more readily taken up and repeated. This is something we financial advisers should always remember.

Done well, categorisation selling in the form of financial sales capitalises on the highly intelligent and highly researched techniques used in retail psychology. It focuses on giving people a better experience when they are 'shopping with you'.

This is, of course, a huge subject, and many interesting studies have been carried out regarding retail psychology and books on the subject of choice. Two I recommend are *The Art of Choosing* by *Sheena Iyengar*[14] and *The Paradox of Choice: Why More Is Less* by Barry Schwartz.[15] Reading these two pieces of work, or further papers on the subject, will enhance your skills and bring you closer to becoming the untouchable, elite sales commando you aim to be.

There is a potential pitfall to categorisation selling that you do need to be aware of and that I would like to mention here. If it's not done correctly, the client may feel like you are spoon-feeding them a little bit too much. If it does all backfire, it may be worth having a miniature reboot of the situation, looking the prospect in the eye and simply saying something like:

You: 'Do you mind if I just break this down into what

---

14   Sheena Iyengar, *The Art of Choosing: The Decisions We Make Everyday of Our Lives, What They Say about Us and How We Can Improve Them,* Abacus, 2011.

15   Barry Schwartz, *The Paradox of Choice: Why More Is Less,* Harper Collins, 2005.

may seem obvious choices for you so that we can both
see that we are absolutely on exactly the same page here?'

Then, slowly lay out the path that is, to you, a series of
obvious choices but that for some reason the prospect's
brain is not following to reach the same destination.
Keep things simple and help the prospect on their way
to the right choice by showing them the map in easy-to-
understand sections.

To be effective in categorisation, each category must
be tackled individually, with its own loaded statement.
For example:

You: 'Do you accept that nothing in the world that
is actually worth having comes for free? Be it health,
fitness, good service or whatever it is you value, there
will always be charges to pay, correct?'

Prospect: 'Yes.'

You: 'Good. So, let's look at what the options are. One,
you could rely on a standard bank account with little,
or no, interest and zero growth on your money. In fact,
compared to inflation, your money is actually shrinking
when left there, agreed?'

Prospect: 'Yes.'

You: 'Option two is a flexible savings plan that allows
some access, maximises your growth and has ultimate
transparency.

'Then there is option three, which is a standard, very
disciplined savings structure that will provide absolutely
no access until the time of maturity. Typically the types

of client that opt for this structure are people who are at a given age, say forty-five to fifty [depending on the prospect's age, you may want to adjust this], and haven't done anything meaningful with regard to their financial futures up to this point. These are the types who know they lack discipline and require a tight corridor to walk along.

'Now, which one of these options suits you best: one, two or three?'

The prospect will pick an option or, even if they don't, they will, at the very least, say they would like to find out more detail before making a decision.

You: 'Okay, great. So we can if needed – and subject to details – look at something other than a standard bank account, agreed?'

Prospect: 'Yes.'

You: 'Perfect.'

And there you have it: your battle plan. By the time you've run through these very compelling options, you should have seen off all but the most stubborn of objection monsters. Of course, it's obviously not a given that this will work every time; however, I will tell you now it is pretty effective in the vast majority of cases. It is certainly a tactic I would recommend adopting and, once again, you can refine it to your own way of working as you become more adept.

Objection-handling: Further set-piece plays

When handling objections, overcoming tricky questions or explaining standard things you know you are going to come across in any given meeting, it is a good idea to have an armoury of set-piece plays that you can rattle off to a prospect. It really helps to think about all the possible questions well in advance and to rehearse and refine your answers, so you deliver them confidently and naturally to your prospect. After all, the quicker, and better, you respond, the less likely it is the objection monster will take hold.

To close this chapter I have listed a range of set-piece plays to handle objections. You are free, indeed positively encouraged, to try some for yourself. I have personally used many of them myself and I have witnessed many others being used on a daily basis by the hundreds of successful financial services sales consultants out there in the field.

Here, in no particular order, are some examples of set ways to answer many of the little wobbles you might get from a prospect.

The positive brush-off

Prospect: 'I don't trust investments.'

You: 'I understand and that's why I'm here. I work on behalf of my clients. I am the guy who walks with you through what can be a rather daunting set of choices. My objective is that we work together to select the solutions that suit you the best and the ones that you are completely happy with too.'

58 WORDS, 21 SECONDS (YOU'RE A PRO)

The cheeky metaphor

Prospect: 'I don't like giving my personal financial details.'

You: 'I totally understand. Let me get this straight, though. When you visit your doctor, do you say to him, "I'm just assessing which doctor to go with right now, but I'm not going to tell you anything about my health." Would you really expect him to give you a full, not to mention accurate, diagnosis on that basis?'

58 WORDS, 19 SECONDS (GET REAL, SIR!)

The third-party story

Prospect: 'I trust my bank, but I have only just met you.'

You: 'Hey, I totally get this. You just need to picture me as someone who is firmly sat in your corner. Let me tell you about a chap I met with last month…'

32 WORDS, 12 SECONDS

Positive categorisation

Prospect: 'I can't meet you tomorrow, I'm too busy.'

You: 'Listen, everyone I deal with is busy. Saying that, though, I'm guessing you will be eating three meals tomorrow, so which one of those meals am I buying you? That way, we can kill two birds with one stone and get this done.'

43 WORDS, 18 SECONDS (NO SIDE-STEPPING YOU!)

Future set-piece framing

Prospect: 'That's all fine. However, I'm never going to stop working.'

You: 'Okay, I get that. Let's imagine, though, that fifteen years ago you started saving just 15 per cent of your money and you had access to all that cash with growth right now. How much better would today feel? Or, think how it would be if 10 per cent of the taxes you paid since you started earning was gifted back to you tomorrow. Imagine the feeling of security and comfort. Think of what we are doing here as taxing yourself before gifting it back to your future self at a certain point in your life. Pretty powerful, huh?'

99 WORDS, 39 SECONDS

Future set-piece framing and categorisation

Prospect: 'That's all fine. However, I'm never going to stop working.'

You: 'If you don't mind, I would like to paint two possible scenarios for you:

'Scenario A: it's ten years in the future and you have saved sensibly, let's say 15 per cent of every dollar you have earned. As a result you have built up a nice nest egg, you know it's there for you to use and it feels like there is a huge safety net underneath you.

'Scenario B: it's ten years from now. However, this time you have, to a greater or lesser degree, continued to run the same patterns that you have been running up until now. You've not been regularly saving, and you've continued to prioritise the immediate and ignored the future, telling yourself everything will be OK tomorrow. As a consequence, you do have slightly more material things in your wardrobe and garage, yet little or no savings to speak of.

'Now, please try to picture these two scenarios, as vividly as possible. Tell me honestly, really honestly, which one would you choose for yourself in a decade's time.'

175 WORDS, 1 MINUTE 14 SECONDS

The hard truth

Prospect: 'What about the risk, though? Isn't my money safe in the bank?'

You: 'Tell me, the bank that you bank with, do they provide credit cards, loans and mortgages? Do they have multiple high-street buildings? Do they carry out marketing with extensive advertising on TV and radio and in newspapers? Do they provide personal loans, student loans and bridging loans? Yes, of course they do.

'Where do you think they get the money to do all this? Yes, from you and millions like you. It's your money. You say your money is "in the bank"; however, it isn't actually in the bank at all. It isn't sat there in the basement with a big armed guard in front of it. No, right now, at this very minute, it's out there funding the plastic credit of millions of random people. If any bank in the world was suddenly asked by everyone who banked with them for their money, it would collapse. The fact of the matter is that you believe your money is safe and you are happy with that state of affairs because that's simply what you have always done. There is no other reason for that false feeling you have of safety, other than the fact it is simply familiar to you. Isn't that the truth?'

204 WORDS, 1 MINUTE 19 SECONDS

The simple process way ahead

Prospect: 'I don't want to provide the details of my friends until I have spoken to them.'

You: 'I completely understand your position. In fact, many people say exactly the same thing to me at this stage, as I'm sure you can imagine. The way we can overcome this is like this: let me know now who you are thinking of speaking to and I will then be able to wash them through our system. If I do this, it will effectively protect and ring fence those people so no one else will contact them. You can then talk to them and, assuming they are happy, you can come back to me and give me the green light. It's only once I get that signal that I will then introduce myself to them. Does that make sense?'

119 WORDS, 43 SECONDS

CASE STUDY
'I only invest in property' objection

This comes up a lot, but, even then, some people are firmer on their beliefs than others. One way of dealing with this objection is to go down the mathematical route and say something like: 'Well, what kind of rent a year are you getting on that property? Do you have any downside capital protection?' Generally, of course, they haven't.

Another tactic is to explain that a property investment is very, very similar to an income loan, the only difference being there's no capital appreciation on the money in an income loan whereas there can potentially be on the property. Also, there isn't a deadline on which it has to be automatically cashed in. However, there are many similarities between the two. Making this link opens the way to going down the route of discussing an income loan. You can say: 'Well, with an income loan, there's no cost of ownership and the yield is equivalent, if not better than, you would get from a property in most markets. It's very cost effective.'

Another route you could go down, particularly if you're sitting with a British client, is that property is a bit more difficult to build into your estate plan, or mitigate in your inheritance tax if you're building up funds. It's much easier to asset-transfer funds, or cash in a plan and put it into a portfolio bond. Remind the client that they are supposed to be trying to make their life a lot more tax efficient in their later years, and providing for retirement when you've got a bunch of properties can be quite complex. That's doubly the case if the properties are spread across various countries.

You've got to really home in on where people's pressure points are. Some people really aren't too bothered about the tax bill that their loved ones are going to have to pay. Others are massively concerned. You've got to probe around and work out where the tipping point is with them. The aim is to demonstrate that you're knowledgeable on this subject from various different angles and give them some food for thought. Ultimately you have to get across the idea that, in the long term, building up this property portfolio and doing nothing else financially is potentially creating a big headache for the client in the future. If you can sow those seeds correctly, you'll be OK.

Duncan Raeside, Senior Wealth Manager

A technical objection is the first refuge of a scoundrel.[16]

16   Heywood Broun, sports writer and newspaper columnist (1888–1939).

Chapter six

ADVANCED TECHNIQUES TO SEE OFF OBJECTIONS

Objections are inevitable, but that doesn't mean they are a door slamming in your face.

The part of the job I enjoy the most is the game or sport of it. When they first meet someone, most sales people spend lots of time trying to build credibility with the prospect so they will trust them. I prefer turning the tables. In some cases I've even said, 'Hold on. I think you must misunderstand the reasons why the meeting has been set up. I'm here because I believe I'm one of the top financial advisers in the area and I can actually help you. That means I will pretty much tell you what it is you should do.'

Sometimes you have to push back a bit to balance things out.

I've also found it really effective that I have literally scripted out all my answers and know them inside out, so I can answer any questions straight away. I use lots of stories, because it is the stories that interest people and that are listened to and remembered. Stories are really very important in sales. I have a story for pretty much everything.

If you achieve a human connection, the rest of it becomes so much easier.

Dave Hughes, Divisional Manager

One sure-fire way to stop the objection monster growing and getting out of hand is to quit jabbering away for a moment and devote some time to understanding just why the person in front of you is resisting your sterling attempts to sell your products. At the very least, even if you do nothing else, you must accept he or she is perfectly entitled to this view. There is certainly no reason to come over all bolshie and aggressive because they haven't immediately signed on the dotted line. It's not your fault (at least it shouldn't be if you've done everything a sales commando should do), but, equally, it isn't their fault either. After all, the person in front of you is almost certainly subject to pressure from all directions all the time. Rest assured, many people other than you will have already made a convincing attempt to part this would-be client from their cash. They may well have heard it all before. It's not always easy to accept, especially when you've worked so hard for this moment, but there is nothing wrong with a prospect taking a firm step back. They are only trying to protect what they have until they are absolutely sure. Be honest – you've probably done the same thing yourself.

If someone is backing off, your job is to find a way to placate their fears without driving them further away and allowing the objection monster to flourish. There are many ideas in the previous chapter on ways to do this, but it may also help to get a better understanding of why the prospect backed off in the first place. Yes, team, we are going to take a step closer to getting inside our prospects' heads with some advanced objection-handling techniques. It's time, as they say in the adverts, to do the science bit.

Let's start gently with a bit of simple psychology. Why do people have objections? Well, we can take it for granted that you haven't completely mis-pitched (presumably you'll already have checked that side of things carefully). Your prospect's reticence could be down to pure and simple, good-old-fashioned resistance to change. Everyone suffers from this – even you. It is human nature and it can happen in any context too, from not wanting to try a new food or visit an unknown venue to hating the idea of working under a new boss. In the context of a financial services pitch, prospects may grow fearful when they consider factors such as:

» the effort that may be involved in setting up their new financial structure
» the potential of any sort of risk or downside
» the need to pay initial costs that they may not completely understand
» how their peers may view their investment decisions.

They may even have convinced themselves they are pretty satisfied with things just the way they are.

The prospect might not say that any one of these things (or indeed all of them) is what is bothering them. Indeed, they probably won't. However, if you are aware of the issues, it won't be too hard to read between the lines to see what is really bothering them.

What is interesting about objections centring around resistance to change is that, in by far the majority of cases, they are in no way connected to the facts of the matter. The reason they have come up is simply because the prospect does not yet feel a compelling enough argument to overcome his internal reservations.

Something you need to be aware of here is not falling into the trap of confusing a resistance-to-change objection with a *condition*. A condition is a completely different proposition.

A condition is a *genuine reason* for the prospect not to buy your product. It may be that the prospect doesn't have any money. If you've done your homework though and pitched your services right, there is actually only a very small number of genuine conditions that could stand in the way of you working together.

The real problems begin when a client panics thanks to the damned resistance-to-change instinct and starts throwing out a confused jumble of objections and conditions. They won't be able to stop themselves coming out with all sorts of excuses, the vast majority of which will have nothing to do with anything you've said, or even what they genuinely feel. This means that, while there may only be a tiny condition or two to get over, these conditions will be hidden by the avalanche of other obstacles and excuses. Do you know what happens then? Unprepared salespeople panic. Worse still, many of them even walk away. Somehow, they convince themselves this prospect isn't worth the bother because they are not going to spend any money anyway. They don't even realise that, by giving up so easily, they are proving to the prospect their objections were right. By walking away at the slightest provocation and not pressing the point home, the salesperson has definitively proved what the prospect suspected – that the salesperson obviously had nothing of real value to offer after all.

A sales commando clearly doesn't give up at the first

hurdle. Or the second. To get on top of the situation, though, the first test to apply is to work out whether the prospect's rebuttal is an objection or a condition. Sometimes it may sound like a condition but if you listen more closely you'll see it is actually an objection.

For example, say the prospect stops you short by saying, 'I can't afford it.'

Don't panic. Delve deeper to see whether what he is actually doing is voicing a resistant objection. The 'it' in his mind may just be his perception of what you're offering, whereas what the prospect actually needs to do is to make a more informed choice. What you initially took to be a condition might only have been an objection based on having too little information. Correct that and you're off to the races.

Are you ready to delve a little deeper now and really see what goes on in your clients' brains?

I'm a big believer that there are two ways to get someone to do something, the hard way and the easy way. The hard way, which is the one that a lot of people use, is to kick the front door down. The other way of going about it, the more consistently successful way, is to actually walk around the back and come in through the window. You can do this if you build up an understanding of what the prospect wants to do. My whole sales technique is geared towards doing that.

My watchword is 'simple'. I do everything I can to keep it simple. When you meet with someone, you are bringing them on a journey from there to there. On that journey there is a whole bunch of hurdles the client has to jump, but you the consultant can dictate how high those hurdles are, or if they even exist at all. The way you do that all depends on how you speak to that person. So, if I speak to someone in a way that they can relate to, there's no hurdle. They just keep walking along with me and I take them through the journey on the simplest possible route. If I speak to them in a way that they don't understand, it just puts a hurdle up.

Noel O'Leary, Executive Director

Left or right brained?

What you can see here is a picture of an adult human brain. (Fig 1) The reason I have included it here is because it is time to start really delving into what makes your prospects tick.

Everyone is, as we all know, different, but, if you look

closely enough, you will discover there are definite trends in the ways people think and react. To get to the bottom of these individual styles, we must tackle the subject of hemispheric dominance, which is science speak for the bit of the brain that determines how we think. Without getting too bogged down in the language of boffins, this is all to do with the cerebral cortex, which is the part of the brain that houses rational functions. The cerebral cortex is divided into two hemispheres connected by a thick band of nerve fibres called the corpus callosum, which sends messages back and forth between the hemispheres. Each of the two hemispheres processes entirely different kinds of information. (Are you keeping up at the back? I'll be asking questions later...)

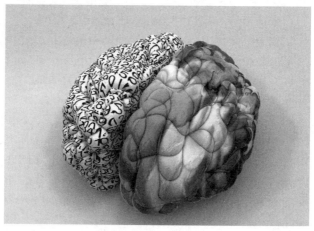

Fig 1

You may have heard the question, 'Are you more left brained or right brained?' This is essentially a simpler way of looking at the science that says each of the brain hemispheres controls a different type of thinking. The left–right question refers to the widely held belief that most people do seem to have a dominant side among the two hemispheres of thought. (It is worth noting here that this is not absolute – we can and do vary our dominant sides, but overall one usually wins out.)

What are these two different processing types? Well, while brain research confirms that both sides of the brain are involved in nearly every human activity, the left side of the brain is the seat of language and processes information in a logical and sequential order. Meanwhile, the right side is said to be more visual and processes material in a more intuitive, holistic and, well, random way.

The origins of this right–left brain theory began with Roger Sperry, who was awarded the Nobel Prize for his work back in the early eighties. He found that, when trying to absorb something that is new, difficult or perhaps even stressful, we each have a preference to learn in a particular way, hence the theory of a dominant side of the brain. Those of us who are more left brained are much more analytical and numeric in their approach, while right-brained folk sometimes rely on what they'd probably call 'gut feeling'.

To understand what all this has to do with how you

might handle objections, let's just look at the two sides in a little more expressive detail. It is my opinion that the key to knowing how to communicate more effectively with your prospect is to recognise which side of the brain they usually favour. This next illustration (Fig 2) should give you some clues.

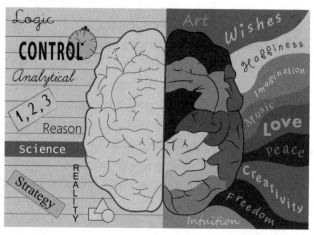

Fig 2

If your prospect is more prone to be left brained, they'll probably agree with the following statements:

» I am a scientist and mathematician and I love the familiar.

» I am accurate, linear, analytical and strategic.

» I am always practical, in control and a master of words and language.

» I am realistic.

» I calculate equations and play with numbers.

» I am order.

» I am logic.

» I know exactly who I am.

Clearly, the left brain has got a lot going on, hasn't it? In fact, it sounds like a left-brained person would make the perfect financial adviser. On a more serious note, though, if you come across a prospect who is pushing hard against the information you are trying to convey in your meeting, it's pretty likely they'll be firing from the left side of their brain.

Let's test that theory, though, and see what the right brain has to say about things.

If your prospect is more prone to being right brained, they'll probably be the type to agree with the following statements:

» I am creative, a free spirit, passionate and sensual.

» I love the feeling of sand beneath my feet.

» I feel the urge to paint on an empty canvas.

» I have boundless imagination and love art and poetry.

» I sense and I feel.

» I am change and evolution.

» I am taste.

» I am movement.

» I am everything I want to be.

Clearly, if you are dealing with a right-brained

person, they'll probably have a very different way of looking at your presentation than their more analytical, information-obsessed, left-brained cousins. Right-brained people are plainly more free spirited and open to change.

This is not all scientific mumbo-jumbo either. This sort of insight is gold dust. If you can recognise how your prospect thinks, you will be able to tailor your pitch to press all the right buttons. Plus, when the prospect comes back with objections, you will be so much more effective at stopping the objection monster in its tracks. Now you know what you are doing, you can deal with a concerned right-brained prospect in a completely different way from how you would respond to a left-brained one who simply wants to drill down into the detail of the figures. If it were clear that your prospect were right brained, you'd have to take into account all sorts of less concrete factors that may make the prospect initially object to your proposal. They may be far more susceptible to emotional concerns, for example, and be distracted by their feelings for their loved ones. They may even be harbouring secret ambitions to do something entirely different with their future, post-retirement. If you understand this might be the case, you can explore the options with them. Can you imagine how powerful that would be? The prospect will love it that you 'get them' and know what makes them tick. A left-brained person, on the other hand, will require a completely different approach.

It may help to look in more detail at how you might deal with each scenario. Let's begin with the logical left brainers and kick off with a problem I call 'left-brain lock'. As we've already seen, the signs will be clear when you come up against a left-brain objection, or lock. Your prospect's objections will primarily be based on needing further information, or time to accurately digest and analyse the information they have already been given.

The first and most essential thing to do is to recognise the objection for what it is. If you are aware that you are dealing with a left-brained person, or someone who is currently operating and processing things with a left-hemisphere dominance (and you should be aware of this simply by hearing the nature of their objections), you'll know you've reached a sticking point simply because you are talking about something – or suggesting a process, solution or course of action – that is not familiar enough to the client to be acceptable without a great deal more analysis on their part. It doesn't matter if what you've been talking about is only slightly unfamiliar, because, in a left-brained person, it will still be enough to cause some degree of blockage. The subject matter you have covered does not utterly synchronise with their existing mind map of the situation and therefore it is being rejected.

If you are lucky, your pitch is not being rejected outright. All being well, your left-brained prospect is merely bringing things to a temporarily halt, or perhaps only slowing them down so they can address each point in their own mind, possibly in their own time. However, this still means their concerns need to be dealt with. You need to get into the labyrinthine corridors of their left brain to get these new ideas flowing freely. If you want to sign this prospect, your mission is to unblock the lock and overcome the hurdle. One way to do this is to take your prospect out of their left-brain mode of thinking and create a moment of right-hemisphere cognitive action. (Don't get nervous here – no brain surgery is involved.)

To get your prospect to take a more right-brained approach, you need to make use of metaphors and visualisations of the future. A metaphor, as you may or may not remember from your school days, is a figure of speech that describes a subject by asserting that it is, on some point of comparison, the same as another otherwise unrelated object. A well-timed metaphor can help your left-brained prospect to 'see' the advantage of working with you to increase their net worth and can be very powerful indeed. Strategically used, metaphors anchor products and services in a left-brained buyer's mind and neutralise their objections, so they see the value over and above the cost.

If your obviously left-brained prospect is struggling, you could say something like, 'Picture yourself at your children's graduation. I bet you'll be feeling pretty proud right then and glad too that you were clever enough to have invested in their education.'

Or, 'You've talked a lot today about your ambitions for the future, but I'm here to tell you that, if you don't plan your future finances, you'll be trying to race a Ferrari without any gas. You just won't get anywhere fast.'

When you use a suitable metaphor, the prospect has to engage right-brain activity to imagine the differing scenario. Once you have invited right-brain activity and the client has engaged, you will immediately be in with a chance of overcoming the obstacle.

If you are going to make use of metaphors, it can give you an added edge to use a comparison that is relevant to the prospect. If they are a golfer, for example, then use golfing analogies. If they are into fast cars, wheel out the Ferrari metaphor. However, while you do want to grab their interest and the easiest way to do it is through something that already inspires their attention, let your prospect work for it a little. As a rule of thumb, the more imagination required to unravel a metaphor the better, if you are trying to get a prospect to overcome an objection.

Another great way of stimulating right-brain activity among our left-brained friends is to simply ask a question along the following lines: 'Okay, I understand you don't agree with/like/accept this, but I wonder whether you can help me to help you. Can we brainstorm a little so you can tell me what would be acceptable to you, if you had everything you wanted from this meeting? Is it possible to give me two, or even three, options you would accept?'

Then, sit and wait with your pen and pad ready to write down their suggestions. You'll be surprised how many times this technique works. I've seen it work brilliantly again and again. The left-brained prospect will go into deep thought as to possible solutions to their own problems and nine times out of ten they usually finish up by coming back to you to ask for your help. Then you have carte blanche to guide them towards the scenario you were steering them towards in the first place. Perfect.

On the other side of the coin to all this is your right-brained prospect. As I have already shown, a prospect who thinks on the right is in many ways pre-programmed to listen to your pitch. As a more free-spirited person, they are more open to change, so if you choose your words carefully and present a convincing argument you'll be halfway there.

Interestingly, though, it is well worth remembering the right-brained person is also far more open to many other visual and vocal cues. If you've never thought much about your body language or vocal inflections before, now is the time to do so. (If you are feeling stuck, go back to chapter two for some ideas.)

I think very carefully about every detail before a meeting. So, for example, being right handed, I always keep the client to my left. I do this because I am quite visual with my hands and, if my hands start waving near their face when I am trying to explain something, they'll naturally pull back. You don't want that sort of barrier and it keeps things natural and relaxed.

Similarly, I always arrange the room so the prospect will have their back to the door. Again, this is to stop them getting distracted by someone walking past or popping their head round. It's quite easy to engineer seating arrangements, even in a large room. I always throw my coat over the chair I want to take and motion them to 'their' seat, saying something like, 'Please take a seat.' You'd be amazed what a difference these small things make.

Chris Withers, Area Manager

A little bit of NLP

To close the chapter, there is one other technique it is well worth considering and that is basic neuro-linguistic programming, or NLP for short. NLP is used a lot in personal development and modern business and is based on understanding how people organise their thinking, feeling, language and behaviour to get things done.

One of the key NLP messages centres on the fact that each of us forms a unique mental map of the world around us, thanks to the way we, as individuals, filter and understand the information we've been given. We absorb that information via our five senses.

Thus, our view of the world is made up of internal images, things we've heard, tactile awareness of stuff we've touched, as well as all the tastes and smells we encounter along the way. Once all this mass of information is received, we assign our own personal 'explanation' to it all, effectively forming a second mental map allotting our own internal images, sounds, feelings, tastes and smells to everything we've absorbed. This second mental map is known as a 'linguistic map'. The 'programming' part of NLP is the behavioural response that occurs as a result of all this information-filtering.

You might well be asking, what does this all mean to me, Doug? Well, just as in the right–left brain scenario, we all filter information in different ways. Some people will take a lot more notice of how things sound, while others will set more store in visual cues. Meanwhile, others will be influenced by how things feel. Knowing stuff like this can give you a real advantage.

If you listen you will hear your prospect give you many clues to the way they think. Take, for example, someone who favours kinaesthetic thought. This means they learn through the tactile sense. If they were a student, they'd prefer to learn by *doing* rather than reading it all in a textbook.

If you were talking to someone whose preferred method of communications was kinaesthetic, you would find they would use certain words or phrases, such as:

» 'This feels/doesn't feel right to me.'
» 'I need a prod to get me to do things.'
» 'Yeah, I grasp what you are trying to say.'
» 'I get the feeling you're going to push me on this.'
» 'I don't like being squeezed or pressurised.'
» 'No, that doesn't really grab me.'
» 'Yeah that feels like it's the sort of thing I'm comfortable with.'

Clearly, all of these reactions relate to touching and feeling. They are typical kinaesthetic thinking indicators. From the perspective of body-language cues, other clues could include them feeling the side of a coffee cup or the pen they have in their hand, or almost stroking a brochure when you hand it to them.

Conversely, if your prospect's preferred method of organising their thinking relied on audio cues, they might well couch their objections with phrases such as:

» 'I don't like the sound of that.'
» 'Listen, I like things like this.'
» 'I hear you.'
» 'Sounds too good to be true.'
» 'Tell me more.'

» 'Okay I'm listening.'

In contrast, a visually orientated person might come back to you with reactions along the lines of:

» 'I like the look of that.'

» 'Looks great.'

» 'I see what you mean.'

» 'That's a bit of a bleak outlook.'

» 'Yes that's clear to me/I'm clear about that.'

Once you know the clues to listen for, you will begin to better understand the NLP style of your prospect. If you are clever you can use this to your advantage to show some empathy with your prospect by tailoring your responses accordingly. So, for example, if you are getting mainly kinaesthetic responses, you can appeal to their tactile side.

> **You:** 'I know you will *feel* a whole lot better once you've finally done something about your pension.' Or: 'Yeah, I hate that *feeling* when you know you should do something but other things get in the way. It *niggles* away, doesn't it?'
>
> Or, if you are dealing with someone who clearly sets great store by what they hear and how they hear it, you should think carefully about your verbal cues. You might like to refer to some of the techniques mentioned at the end of the previous section and pay extra attention to adjusting your spoken intonation accordingly.

If I can tell a client is very visual, I always use metaphors to connect with them and explain things better. One of my favourites is based on the fact that one of the biggest assets most people have is their house. That's what they're determined to put the most money into, regardless of whether it is the best thing for them. I always say, 'That's fine, but I can't imagine you all sat around the table at Christmas saying, "Right then, which brick shall we eat?"'

It always gets a laugh, but it makes the point. It's great to put all your money into a house, but you can't eat bricks. This picture really brings it home to people.

Steve Rigby, Divisional Manager

If you really tune into your client and tailor your responses to how they think, rather than how you think they should think – or, even worse, imagining that one size fits all – you will be amazed at how much more of your communication is readily taken up by the prospect.

I will add one note of caution. NLP is a huge subject and there are whole books, seminars and lengthy courses devoted to it. I won't pretend we've done anything other than scratch the surface here. If you are interested in exploring the subject in more depth, I would recommend doing some further reading. Two books I rate are *Selling with*

NLP [17] and NLP: *The New Art and Science of Getting What You Want.*[18]

If, on the other hand, you chose to merely dabble in NLP, don't fall into the trap of haring off in one direction after you've only heard one or two words that you take to be clues to how your prospect thinks. I would strongly advise against doggedly pursuing one course of behaviour on this basis. Remember, simply hearing one or two words from a certain thought mode does not necessarily mean the person is that way dominant. We all can and do use all of these terms at different points in our lives – indeed we do so nearly every day. If you are going to take advantage of NLP techniques, you must at the very least develop your skills in cross-referencing verbal cues so you can assess the right signposts *before* you rush to judgement.

NLP, like all of the behavioural observations and techniques outlined in this chapter, will take time to learn and patience and perseverance to perfect. It is my strong view that it is well worth devoting some time to understanding the client's input into the sales process and in particular the objection process, because, the more fully you know their drivers and motivation, the better you'll be able to stop any objections in their tracks. Once you've mastered these simple yet profound

17   Kerry L. Johnson, *Selling with NLP: Revolutionary New Sales Techniques that Will Double Your Volume*, Nicholas Brealey Publishing, 1994.
18   Harry Alder, *NLP: The New Art and Science of Getting What You Want*, Piatkus, 1995.

techniques to unlock what your prospect is really thinking, you'll be able to speak to them in the language of their own minds. This can open up entirely new and more powerful way of selling to them.

By learning the skills to become a detective of human behaviour, you'll understand how the person in front of you makes their decisions to buy – or, just as importantly, what might influence them *not* to buy. You'll also be able to use simple physical and verbal techniques to reinforce the trust between you and develop a much better understanding and rapport. Do this well and objections will turn into approval. Every time.

Human behaviour is incredibly pliable, plastic.[19]

---

19   Philip George Zimbardo, psychologist and professor emeritus at Stanford University, USA(1933–).

Chapter seven

REFERRALS: THE OBVIOUS PATH TO TAKE

Take time to master the art.

The road to a sale is a long and winding one. For many people, the primary objective of the whole process is to get the client to take up a savings plan, financial product or investment of some kind. But, if you are one of those people and the scale of your ambitions end there, you will never, ever join the ranks of the sales elite.

If you want to be a sales commando, referrals should be your focus in every single meeting you have. Without a doubt. If you are truly committed to the path of least resistance to success, with deeper, faster traction that keeps you well ahead of the pack, then this is the way to go. A well-planned referral strategy *will* guarantee you optimum velocity as soon as possible and is the route to the very top of the sales mountain.

Actually no. It is more than that. A steady stream of referrals is the express cable car, first class route with VIP service all the way to the summit.

Your mission is to sell yourself in such a way that you constantly and relentlessly remind your client you are referable and that you work from referrals. You must never miss the opportunity to drop this vital fact into the conversation. Leave your client in no doubt – you thrive on like-minded individuals.

As sales commandos we need to be able to sell to the builder and the barrister and everyone in between, so we must be super-confident in the way we handle our weaponry. Training, rehearsing and drilling the techniques is the way to become elite. That's why you're here, right?

In this chapter and the next we will look at the most powerful elements of salescraft and weapons you can put into your armoury to guarantee referrals. These weapons are there to help you keep safe, protect your career and make you victorious at what you do.

Each of these weapons has been fashioned on the battlefield of sales. They have been born from the front line and are used around the world very successfully. They are like all good weapons, too: simple, yet ruthlessly effective.

Learn how to use all the weapons I will show you

here. Rehearse them, train in them, role-play them and become super-confident at using them *all*.

The weapons you are going to learn in this section absolutely work when executed professionally and, the more of them you deploy in each meeting, the more chance you have of achieving your objective. In these two chapters, I will give you all the best referrals techniques and weapons I have witnessed and used. It is up to you which ones you opt to use, or whether you adopt them all and pick and choose which one will be most effective and when.

Why do you need to do this?

Well, referrals rock because:

» A credible third party who has experienced first hand the mind-blowing advantages of doing business with you is going to be your best ambassador ever. Their friends and colleagues will count on the fact your client has no ulterior motive and will take it for granted they are only acting in their best interests. After all, who wouldn't be more likely to believe what someone close to them says rather than a mere salesperson who might only be motivated by making a quick buck?

» If you set up a meeting as a result of a referral, the meeting automatically begins far higher up the buying and decision-making chart. It is simply much easier to take the prospect the rest of the way to conclusion.

» They are completely free. Get it right and you'll be getting the benefit of the best sales advert ever, for absolutely nothing. What's not to like?

» They tie your existing clients to you too. Yes team, once you've got your current clients to metaphorically stand up and say you are the best, psychologically they will become more loyal to you and your business too. It's a win–win situation.

» When you attend a referred meeting with a prospect, you are, statistically speaking, far more likely to gain further referrals and introductions from that particular meeting. They know how it works. Boom.

Actively seeking referrals is the obvious path to take. So, why doesn't everyone do it? As a sales mentor, it drives me nuts when I see all these wasted opportunities. I've sat with so-called sales professionals who get uncomfortable when I mention referrals. They mutter something about the fact they 'kinda try', or 'sorta have a go', or (and this is my personal pet hate) they 'get them where they can'. What they are really saying is: 'I can't really be bothered with actively seeking referrals, but if the client gives them to me anyway, that's great.'

Well, that's a pretty go-getting attitude, isn't it? Hmmm, let me see. Er, no, it bloody well isn't.

I won't kid you here. Seeking out referrals takes application, guts and determination. You'll sometimes have to ask the question in situations that will be uncomfortable and a lot of the time it will seem a lot easier to avoid the potential pain of rejection.

But, we are not here to take the easy way out. We're here to become sales commandos and, if it gets a bit tough along the way, well that is just how we like it.

So let's do this and do this well. Let's focus on being referable and leveraging our relationships. Let's get to the very top and celebrate our success. Let's nail life to the wall and dominate this space.

A breakfast lesson

I once conducted a small breakfast meeting with six clients who all worked for the same large construction group. As we all ate our breakfast and chatted I was asked a general question by one of the six clients. My answer emboldened the other clients there to dig a little deeper and debate the given subject further and sparked a round-table questioning session that I hadn't really expected. I have to say, at times I was tested. I was also surprised at some of the queries because, in my mind, the subjects had been thoroughly covered in previous meetings with the individual clients.

I walked away from that breakfast with the realisation that, while I may have assumed the clients understood certain things about the products and services and the way I personally worked, it did not necessarily follow that they actually did. After all, just because this was my world, it didn't mean it was everyone else's.

Openly discussing and cross-referencing things, while of course maintaining individual confidentiality, was a powerful learning experience for my clients, who benefited hugely from it. Another benefit was that it reinforced for those clients how important and valuable it was to work with me. After all, they had been surrounded by a group of influential peers at *my* breakfast. It was a beneficial and powerful experience for them and, after that, the numbers in that circle grew exponentially.

This was a real game-changer for me. I had had to work extremely hard to get the first few clients in that group to refer me to their peers. They had put up loads of barriers and it didn't come easily, but, once I had made this breakthrough and the clients actually got it and truly recognised there were tangible benefits to them in introducing me to other people, the floodgates opened. My clients were delighted to refer me to people they knew and trusted. It became a pleasure.

After this experience, I thought about how I could replicate it across my client base. I concluded the best way was to simply tell them the story and make it funny by being a little self-deprecating regarding being put under pressure by my clients. I showed it was a very powerful thing for my clients if I dealt with a number of people they were close to. It worked brilliantly. Most clients and prospects were happy to hear about how others like them interacted with me and benefited from the best possible service.

EXERCISE
Learn to believe in yourself and your power of persuasion

If you know in your heart you are 100 per cent referable, the rest is easy. You must make great efforts every day to think in the right way. When you think in the right way you act in the right way, when you act in the right way you behave in the right way and when you behave in the right way you become that person. Think, act, behave, become, think, act, behave, become!

Step one: Picture, in your mind's eye, a sales consultant who is in your opinion completely and utterly unreferrable. Maybe they are a bit grubby around the edges. Perhaps they smoke too much and always go into a meeting reeking of cigarettes. Maybe they are just a bit rude or abrupt. Or, they could even be a mixture of all of these things. Take a moment to get a real feel for this person. Use all your senses to imagine how they smell, how grating their voice sounds and how unkempt they look. Now, imagine what would happen if someone like this went into a meeting and asked for a referral. Without a doubt, the prospect will be thinking, 'Refer you to my friends? Are you joking? I can't wait to see the back of you.'

Step two: Picture the opposite of this odious consultant. This fellow will dress sharply and will have wit and humour to match. He'll carry himself with confidence and pay utmost attention to every aspect of his dress and demeanour, right down to the tone of voice he uses, the cut and cleanliness of his suit, the crisp cologne he wears and his confident, yet approachable, way of speaking.

Think about a scale of sales consultant from one to ten; the scruff-bag from step one would be a zero while this fellow would without doubt be a clear ten. (And, rest assured, when you go into a meeting with a client, he or she will instantly place you on this scale.) It is your mission to make sure you are always a ten, because a ten means the client won't be able to stop themselves thinking and talking highly of you. In fact, they'll be so impressed, they won't be able to help themselves becoming evangelists out there in the marketplace, singing your praises.

Take charge of yourself. Every day, before you go to work, imagine yourself as the consultant described in step two. When you slip on your smart, well-pressed, suit, picture that outfit as an invisible suit of armour that clothes the perfect consultant. Hold yourself like that ten, walk like him, talk like him and pay attention to every detail. At first this new strong suit may not fit you exactly. It will pinch in places, like a tight pair of new shoes. However, in time, if you persist, you will start to become this person. You will become more comfortable with this new ultra-professional you.

Think like a pro. Act like a pro. Then you will become a pro. Create another you that dominates your work and your industry. It is the sales commando way.

Referrals are the objective – from beginning to end

CASE STUDY
Added value, easy as one, two, three

I cover the referrals process right from the beginning, by putting it under point one of the agenda, which is an introduction to my company. I outline in detail what we do and how we get paid.

I say something like, 'People always ask how we get paid and I say we actually get paid twice. The first time is through the institutions we work with and the second one, which I personally feel is very important, is at the end of a meeting like this.'

At this stage the client may be looking puzzled. So, I tell them it is all about value. Taking a pad, I write down what I think value is:

1. Value is, after we've had the meeting, I find out nothing is wrong with the client's financial situation, so I can put their mind at rest.

2. Or, perhaps, they learn something that may be of use to them either now or in the future.

3. Or, we find an issue, or issues, we can address to actually improve their financial situation.

I reiterate that this is what I define as value and say that if, at the end of the meeting, the client believes he or she has got value like this, I would like them to introduce me to three or four people they know who would also benefit from this sort of value. I ask them,

'Are you prepared to go ahead on this basis?'

Everyone says, 'Yes.'

At the end of the meeting I always ask, 'Did you get value?'

The answer is always 'yes', so I drill down into the answer and ask what part of the meeting they got value from. This is their opportunity to tell me which parts they liked.

I then spin the piece of paper around that was our contract and terms of business and say, 'Remember this? You said you got value here today and earlier you told me that if you did you would introduce me to three or four people.'

Some people will immediately say, 'Okay, fine,' and provide the introductions. However, some others will say they are not comfortable with it and want to 'wait and see'. I come straight back at them and immediately say, 'Well that's not what *you* agreed.'

I put the physical evidence in front of them and point to the part we talked though right at the beginning. The usual comeback from this is, 'Yeah, well I'm still not comfortable.'

I don't give in, though. I say, 'I promised you all of this – service, resources, best solution and everything else. How would you feel if I promised you all that and then didn't deliver?' They will have to admit they'd feel pretty bad, so I ask them how they think I feel.

This is the point when nine out of ten people crumble.

Andrew Oliver, Senior Area Manager

Looking for referrals has to start from the minute you walk into the meeting. Indeed, even before the first handshake you can begin the process by suggesting you work in this way when you set up the appointment itself.

From that moment on, you must constantly drop hints. You need to weave into the actual groundwork of your very presentation the fact that you are referable and that you work from referrals. It is vital to drive the point home that this is the way everyone you deal with works, so that your clients regularly refer you on to other like-minded individuals.

Don't just figure on bolting on a brief referrals pitch at the end of your presentation and then expect the prospect to pop up with the goods. That's never going to work. Your task is to keep coming back to the idea of referrals throughout the whole hour or so you spend with your client.

Don't ever miss a trick. When, for example, you enter the meeting, ask about the person who just passed you in reception. When the prospect tells you their name, smile and say, 'Ah good, I'll get their details from you at the end. I can probably help them too. Anyway, good to meet you, how's the day going?'

Then, almost immediately, work into the discussion the fact that you have just come from a meeting with another potential client who was put in front of you via an existing client of yours. Add that this is typically the way you go about meeting new people.

'It's simply the most comfortable way to do business,' you can tell the prospect confidently.

As the meeting progresses, ask the prospect how the company they work for gets new contracts, orders or customers. Even if the person you are meeting is hidden away in the admin or technical departments, they will be familiar with the concept that the company they work for requires a constant stream of new orders to grow. That is, after all, what will sustain their own careers. Listen to what they tell you and keep a careful note of their answers. Build a dialogue from there to explain how you personally work to gain new business.

At every twist and turn and at every opportunity, infer referrals. Your approach doesn't have to be completely in their faces. As you get better at it, you can be quite subtle some of the time (but only if the message is obviously getting through), so the concept of introductions is taken up almost subliminally by the prospect.

Get yourself into a mindset in which you look upon getting referrals as simply another part of the sales process. Look at it this way: when you are selling anything, you will always endeavour to put yourself in a position in which you can narrow the gap between where your prospect is now and where you'd like them to be. It'll be much easier for your prospect to make that leap of faith if you create a nice solid bridge for them to walk across, by dropping in easy-to-digest comments and statements; that way, the bridge is built brick by brick. If you do the groundwork well, it will make it an easy decision for them and it won't be such a huge leap of faith at all.

The end of the meeting is just as important as the beginning, too. After all, what are the two moments you remember most when you meet someone for the first time? The beginning and the end, of course. Yet, there are far too many times when I have witnessed consultants literally rushing away from meetings. These consultants seem to make no real effort to effectively land the prospect during the meeting. To reiterate, you have taken them from a static position and encouraged them to come on a journey with you, you've shown them new heights and suggested various eventualities for their financial futures and you have injected energy and emotion at all the right times to navigate and, at times, overcome certain situations. At this moment, settling them back down with rapport and perhaps some laughter is essential, as is gaining commitment to referrals. Yet, some people let the prospect just drop out of the sky and crash. Not good.

There are lots of great ways to end a meeting and secure the idea of referrals in your prospect's mind. One of my personal favourites is to show my prospect just how passionate I am about my job by telling them just that. I'll also be sure to talk with conviction about a particular subject, such as the pension crisis. If you speak convincingly and knowledgeably, it is a sure-fire way to leave your prospect thinking, 'Wow, that person really believes in their job.' Look to use stories that you personally like that are relevant.

In the past, I've also used this method very effectively to break down a sceptical prospect. If you speak with true conviction, it quickly destroys their defences and gets them listening on a level that is more conducive to doing business.

You might also think about establishing a routine that will ensure you don't ever forget to ask for introductions following your consultation. Doing so is also a great way to obtain instant (and hopefully positive) feedback from your meeting. It will also lead the prospect into taking the action you want in providing introductions.

One way of doing this goes something like this.

Following your consultation, fully open up your Fact Find and lay it before the prospect. If they don't have a pen close by, hand them yours.

> **You:** 'Now, because I love to get feedback, could you tell me the parts of the consultation you got the most from?'

Invite them to use the pen to tick or mark off in some way the points they agree with. This physical connection with the process is very important because it ties them still closer with what you've been saying. Give them the time and space to expand further on what they have experienced and how they feel about it. If you have done your job right, there will be some positive feedback.

It is a good idea to get them to sign and date the Fact Find to confirm that all the information they've been given is indeed correct. This act alone is extremely powerful.

Now, all you need to do is turn the page or point to the section that requests introductions and ask them to complete it as agreed. If you keep a separate book, or journal of some kind, open it up and ask them to add to it.

Sometimes, this moment can be a little sticky or awkward. The way to get around this is to hold the client's hand and coach them through it. The process could go something like this.

> **You:** 'Okay, we talked about thinking of people that I would get on with and who would benefit from my advice, so let me help you with this process.'

Then, immediately, move onto the picture book method. Taking a separate pad of paper, draw a number of squares. Then, label each one of them individually, according to what you have learnt about this person's life. One of their areas of focus might be golf, another their child's school, another work colleagues and so on. Your aim is to get the names of two referrals in each box.

> **You:** 'Picture the last couple of games of golf you had. Who were they with?'

At this point, all being well, you will see the prospect start to think. They will look away from you and stare into the middle distance as they visualise the moment. When they have pictured their most recent game, they will regain eye contact and come back on-line.

> Client: 'Ah, Fred. Yeah, Fred's a good one.'
>
> You (writing the name 'Fred' in the golf box): 'Great. Anyone else?'

All you need to do then is just repeat that process. Don't get too locked into details at this stage. You only need their first names. The idea is to help the prospect in front of you to start walking up the path.

Only once the box matrix is full and you are satisfied you've exhausted all the possibilities should you go on to fill in the details. Now, you can work on adding in the surnames and as much detail as you can get.

> You: 'What's Fred's surname? And how will I get hold of him?'

If your prospect seems reluctant, or stalls, say the first few numbers of Fred's mobile and they'll usually come right back with the full thing.

> You: 'Is Fred's number 07…'
>
> Client: 'No, it's 09078…'

Another way of doing this is as follows.

> You: 'Let's get some more details for these people. I'm guessing they'll all be on your mobile phone. So, what are their numbers?'

Then, once the client has given you the details, re-affirm to them that you will only contact their friends and colleagues after they themselves have spoken to them. You may want to be a little light-hearted at this point and drop in the fact that obviously you'll only call these people after your client has sung your praises and done all the hard work.

Once you have this finished this process, make sure you acknowledge it fully and say how much you appreciate it. Then enter your closing-off phase of the meeting, rapport them down and exit.

I always finish a meeting with a general overview of the client's situation and that allows me to document where the client is and what they're doing. I explain it is a compliance exercise for me to make sure that every bit of advice I give is correct. Then, I fold up the paperwork, or turn it over, and say, 'In terms of how we get paid, whether you go directly to the institution or whether you come through us, there is no extra cost to you, but you will get all those extra services and guidelines I've just been telling you about. What I do ask for is the names and numbers of people that you know that you think could potentially be interested in a level of service like this.'

I reassure them that they may not know the financial situations of their families, friends or colleagues but that neither do I right now. There is no reason for the client to panic, though, because I am just trying to help people they know with professional advice.

Andrew Lockyer, Senior Consultant

Activating existing clients to give referrals

I'll never, ever, understand not gaining referrals when you've signed someone up. I just don't get it. There's somewhere in my brain that doesn't let that compute, because that says to me that someone's ethos is not quite right. Personally, I think referrals are an entirely value-based system. They're purely and absolutely based on your value of yourself and your own self-worth.

If you think you're good at what you do, you should expect them, because you shouldn't work for free.

Therefore, go for the line of least resistance: the one time that a client is more likely to give you a referral than anywhere else is in the presentation. That's when you have the relationship and they're doing business with you. That is the greatest affirmation anyone can ever give to you in our industry. It is when they say to you, 'I'm going to invest my money with you.' So, to not actually use that opportunity to say, 'Who else can I help?' is, to me, a sign of a weak adviser. It's someone who either doesn't value themselves or is not really in this industry for the long term.

Noel O'Leary, Executive Director

Let's give a little time to sparking a little life out of your existing clients. These are techniques you can use straight away with the bank of clients you already have, or perhaps ones who are new to you if you've recently joined a new brokerage and/or inherited some clients.

In this situation, it is quite likely you will have a number of clients who, for whatever reason, do not actively help you meet other potential new clients. It could be because you, or the person who originally took them on, didn't properly manage their expectations. The foundations of the way the relationship between you is going to work may not have been laid out correctly. Or, perhaps, the clients were simply signed up and never really asked for introductions. I call clients who fall into this category 'untrained'.

An alternative scenario is when you (or whoever originally won the client) did at least attempt to discuss referrals but never really saw the approach through to a satisfactory conclusion. The point was never properly pressed home that you work off referrals. There may have been many reasons for this, but most of the time the sticking point boils down to some sort of ill-founded fear it will somehow blow the whole deal. I call this category the 'lost'.

The third possibility is that, in spite of you or your colleagues doing everything possible, the client is simply not wired that way and just doesn't want to, or will not, refer you (yet!). I call this category the 'bullet proof'.

Whatever the reason for this lack of action among your existing client base, the outcome remains the same. By continuing with the status quo, you will be pouring valuable time, energy and resources into a client base that is not benefiting your mission in any way. You are being busy yet extremely unproductive. This is not a state of affairs any sales commando should be prepared to tolerate.

It's time to knock the clients you do have into shape and start getting the referrals you so richly deserve. To begin this mission, we need to identify, with total clarity, which of the unproductive categories each person in your client bank fills. Are they:

» *Untrained*, which means they have not been asked or educated about the importance of referrals and therefore the situation is not their fault.

» *Lost,* which is the equivalent of them being in the classroom when the lesson was being taught, but you (or another salesperson) poorly executed the lesson itself. In short, you, or whoever went before you, didn't truly go for it.

» *Bullet proof,* meaning attempts have repeatedly been made to educate the client using experience, passion and logic, but they just won't budge.

Devote as much time as is necessary to thoroughly checking each of your clients against this list. It is an exercise well worth doing because it is only once you have done it properly that you'll be able to develop a plan of attack to convert these hitherto neglected opportunities into active recruiters for you.

The next stage of this process is to call up each of your clients in turn and arrange a meeting with them. Mention to each one that you have something important to discuss with them. It's important to do this at an early stage, because it builds up a small amount of expectation around the coming meeting. This will ensure your client is primed to 'set up their listening' correctly.

Then, when it comes to the meeting itself, depending on what category individual clients fall into, re-approach the subject in a way that is meaningful and powerful for them. The following sections contain some pointers as to how to tackle the meeting for each of the three categories.

The untrained

For the sake of the following example, let's call the client Jane.

> **You** (following the usual greeting and opening rapport): 'Jane, today I want to discuss with you something that I realise I have neglected to inform you about in our previous meetings. It's regarding the way I grow my business and the policies I adopt to ensure I'm giving a great service to everyone and working productively. Would it be OK with you to spend some time on this?'
>
> **Jane:** 'Yeah, sure.'
>
> **You:** 'Jane, if I may ask, what is your understanding about the way I actually get paid?'
>
> **Jane:** 'Well, I suppose you get some kind of wage and you also get some form of commission from the company when you gain more customers, right?'
>
> **You:** 'Yeah, that's about right, Jane, but mainly I am remunerated by introducing new clients to financial institutions. Effectively, I broker deals and the institution remunerates the company, which in turn pays me. To put it simply, that's how I feed the family.
>
> 'Now, while we are talking about this, may I also ask you, Jane, what you believe to be the best way for me to meet new people so I can continue to grow my client base and drive my income forwards?'
>
> **Jane:** 'Um, well, advertising? Er, phoning people up and getting people to introduce you to others, I suppose.'
>
> **You:** 'Perfect. If you were in my shoes, what would be

the way that you would personally prefer to meet new people?'

Jane: 'Well, via personal introduction I guess.'

You: 'That's right, Jane, and that's what I want to talk to you about today.'

Jane: 'Okay.'

You: 'So, Jane, what's the best way that I can get to meet some people in your world? Should I just call them up, take you all out for breakfast or lunch, or shall we have a round of golf together? What do you think is the best way for us to produce this outcome?'

(If you are a fee-based adviser, then please adjust your response accordingly.)

With this approach, you really don't need to go through a hundred different reasons why the 'untrained' client should give you referrals. Well, not straight away anyway, because that would be over-egging it, wouldn't it? Hammering away at all the reasons would feel like over-selling to your client and might alarm them. However, by introducing referrals in this relaxed way, 'Jane' gets to work out for herself what you are after, Even better, she's vocalised that she herself would operate in that way if she were you. All you need to do is to allow her to use her own mind within the framework you have set out and half the battle is won. Now you can work together to firm up the details of those new introductions.

The lost

For the 'lost', who didn't get 'educated' about referrals the first time around, we'll go down a fairly similar route to the 'untrained'. However, in this case, we'll open things up a little differently and be prepared for a small amount of resistance along the way.

In the following example, we'll call our fictitious client Mike.

> **You:** 'Mike, may I ask, what is your understanding of how I actually get paid?'
>
> **Mike:** 'Well, you get a commission on new business, don't you?'
>
> **You:** 'Yes, that's right. Bearing this in mind, I carried out an interesting exercise a few weeks ago. It revolved around my productivity and effectiveness within my daily workload. Can I seek your advice because I'd value your input?'
>
> **Mike:** 'Yeah, sure.'
>
> **You:** 'How would you go about meeting the right people to advise if you were doing my job?'

Then, allow Mike to answer. The nature of his answers will obviously shape your response, but it's extremely rare in this scenario that the client won't mention introductions via existing clients in some way. As soon as they do mention existing clients, this is the time for you to jump back in.

> **You:** 'That's right, Mike, and you know by far the most effective way to do business is through meeting

people via other people I already serve. It's specifically this I want to talk to you about today, Mike. I want to brainstorm with you a little and come up with, say, three options or ideas about how I could go about meeting some of the people you know that I don't. You know what I do and how I work, so just think about the kind of people that you believe I would get on with. Does that make sense?'

Mike: 'Yeah, I guess.'

You: 'Awesome. What do you think about ways I can meet them? Should I call them up? Or would you recommend that I take them to dinner, lunch or breakfast with you? I'm happy to pay for a round of golf. What do you think would be best? I'm all ears.'

The bullet proof

The 'bullet proof' guys might seem like tough nuts to crack. After all, they've already proved spectacularly resistant to the idea of referrals. You have, in your opinion, given them your best performance and yet they still haven't budged an inch. Even more frustratingly, they may have gone through the motions, promising to come up with the goods when they've been in front of you in an elaborate charade of appearing to appease you. Then, when push comes to shove, all they produce is lame excuses.

This means a more robust approach is required. In the following scenario, the client will be called Alex.

You: 'Alex, a few weeks ago I sat down and carried out an interesting exercise. It was all to do with my productivity and effectiveness within my daily workload. I drew up a list of all my clients and simply characterised them into A-list and B-list clients. The A list were people who totally understood how I grow my network and get paid and the B list were people who didn't. May I ask, what list do you think I placed you on?'

The answer they give will indicate just how hard you have to try here. They may say A or B, but, either way, I would seek clarification on their perception of the way you get paid and grow your network.

Then, if they have answered A, simply ask why they choose to not assist you in growing your network. If it's B give some time to re-educating them as to all the ways you get paid and grow your network.

Then go on to say:

You: 'After I did my A and B lists, I further categorised people into two more lists, the red and greens. The green list is for the people who totally get how I work and value my service. I can rely on the fact that, every now and again, when I go to see someone on a green list, they are ready and waiting with a couple of names written down on a piece of paper for me. These names will be colleagues and/or friends they have spoken to favourably about me in my absence and who are happy for me to give them a call to introduce myself.

'Then there is the red list. The red list contains the people that, no matter how much they fully understand the way I work, have not as yet yielded any positive introduction. Not one. In fact, they never really assist me in any way whatsoever in growing my network.

'I'm sorry to say that you are on the red list, Alex, and I truly don't want you to be there. I mean, if you were me and you were trying to work as effectively as possible, who would you rather go and see? Which client would you always go that extra yard for? The reds or the greens?'

Alex: 'Well the greens.'

You: 'Yeah, that's right. So, come on Alex, help me to help you. Tell me what I have to do to get you on the green list, because I want you to get the premium service going forwards. What do I have to do to make it as comfortable as possible for you to help me grow? Do I have to take you and your friends out for dinner, lunch or breakfast? Come on, how can we do this? What would work best for you?'

As the conversation unfolds, the key to success is to really believe and have conviction in your words. Really emphasise each syllable of the question when you are asking what the best way is that you can help the prospect to help you. You are trying, though your impassioned plea, to make them tell the bloody truth.

It's important you really feel that passion, too. Look at your clients and think about how they haven't made any effort to benefit you or help in any way. Add up the man-hours, petrol, vehicle wear and tear and sheer energy you've placed into looking after them year after year. If it helps, put a price on your time and realise what it costs you. Get yourself totally motivated to re-approach this subject with them and find a solution to the part of your game that is haemorrhaging potential.

What to do now!

Right now, you should be thinking about each of your clients and how you are going to approach them to make sure they give you the referrals you need to grow your business. Take each technique in turn, rehearse them, role-play them and then go out and execute them in a real-life scenario. Then, do it again and again until you perfect your approach. It will work time and again. Pretty soon you'll be wondering why you never did it before.

So, what are you waiting for?

Never, ever, lose sight of the fact that referrals are, without a doubt, the fastest way to the top.

Chapter eight

THREE POWERFUL WEAPONS TO GUARANTEE REFERRALS EVERY TIME

Asking for referrals is a natural part of the sales process.

CASE STUDY
Adapt your referrals pitch to the circumstances

I always tell clients my job is easy now I'm established. I lose maybe thirty of my clients every year and I replace those thirty clients purely via referrals and recommendations.

If I want to be sneaky about it, I'll say, 'Most of my clients really understand the importance of referrals and really help me. That's great because they get invited to golf days and whatever else we have on. I thank them like that because I'm really appreciative.'

Then, I pause and say, 'There is about 20 per cent who always say they'll give me referrals, but for some reason they don't. I don't get it because I give them exactly the same service. Still, 80 per cent of my clients really look after me and I'm massively thankful for that.

'Referrals are really important to me, but all I ask for is fairness. If I do a good job I'm pretty sure you'll just give me referrals anyway. I shouldn't even have to ask for them. If someone does me a good job I just want to help them because I respect that person and what they do.'

At the end of the meeting, when I ask for referrals, I ask them with a laugh whether they want to be like the 20 per cent. This always makes them feel a bit awkward, so they nearly always give me referrals.

My pitch does change every time I speak to someone, though. It's never the same. I've got various examples and I just mix it up so it's more like a conversation.

So, yesterday I sat with somebody and I said, 'It's great that I'm sitting here because I work referral only. I've been helping your colleague here and this other colleague there and it's important for me to work that way.

'The way I see it is, I could have sat with you in a bar, or we could've been at a barbecue at the weekend. You might have thought I'm a great guy and liked me, but you wouldn't know I'm good at my job. The great thing about referrals is, before we've even sat down, there's an element of trust that you know I'll do a good job. If I didn't do a good job, why would your colleagues have introduced us?

'If I'd had a kitchen fitted and was in the pub and someone said, 'Does anyone know a kitchen fitter?' I'd be first one putting my hand up if my guy had done a good job. I'd be saying, 'You need to phone this guy, let me give you his number.' I'd want to give out his number. If he did an average job, I probably wouldn't recommend him, and for a below-average job I certainly wouldn't recommend him.

I get all that in straight away. Then I just keep nipping away at it.

Graham Bentley, Senior Area Manager

I would like to kick off this chapter by spending a few moments making sure you are up to speed with some of the terminology I use here and, in particular, that you fully understand the difference between an objective and a scenario, because your confidence and flexibility here are essential. For anyone who is not sure, these are the definitions:

» The *objective* is the game plan. It is the battle order driving you towards the ultimate outcome you are striving to achieve.

» The *scenario* is the conditions in which you are attempting to achieve that objective.

As most people are aware, no battle ever fought goes exactly to plan. Whenever you set out to achieve a given objective, the scenario can change at any moment. It can make the attempt more difficult, or in some cases well-nigh impossible, so you should always have a backup plan, a default option or a plan B to strive for when achieving your primary objective becomes impossible.

You can also decide when to abort your primary and move to your secondary, if needs be and if the primary doesn't have the desired effect. You are the soldier on the ground, so you are the one who is in charge of making the right call.

Obviously this means it is essential to have a primary *and* a secondary objective for every aspect of the sales cycle. You must also be drilled and organised in the way you are going to carry your strategy out and know exactly what possible scenario changes you could come up against that would require you to change the way you are working.

So, what might those objectives be? In the case of referrals, the primary and secondary objectives during a first-appointment scenario with a potential client might be something like this:

» Primary: to gain firm introductions at the first meeting.
» Secondary: a firm agreement to gain introductions via a personal meeting, with a set time period attached.

Clearly, when you are in a meeting situation, many things can happen. It is even possible you'll inadvertently place a foot wrong in any direction and change the scenario from good to bad. Nevertheless, if you are prepared, you'll quickly recognise this fact and push on with your objective, although possibly with a slightly adjusted stance.

It is most important that you are always battle alert and ready to jump on top of any changes in direction. In sales there are always difficulties along the way that must be overcome. That is part of the job. If you come up against your first objections and difficulties, don't panic and change the pitch completely or, even worse, give up altogether and surrender. Then you are not a true sales commando. You are not elite. You are acting like cannon fodder and will be treated as such. Push hard for your objectives in all scenarios, follow and adjust your plan, and stick to intelligent choices. If you find yourself floundering too easily at objections and slipping from one technique to another with no obvious strategy, go back through chapters five and six before moving on.

A big part of this referrals strategy is to master these weapons and elements of salescraft so well they are locked in your unconscious competence. You should be able to pick any of them up and use them without thinking, slipping flawlessly from one to another as the pitch situation ebbs and flows.

Do this right and you'll know every weapon so well

it will become second nature to know the perfect time to use each and every technique. You'll be able to handle each one like the true sales professional you are. To be able to do this takes practice. If you try to use these techniques for the first time in the actual sale, the chances are they will not be effective. If you're good (and very lucky), you'll probably be able to wing it and follow a script, but it'll never be perfect and the slightest deviation will floor you. If it is not instinctive – if you haven't gone over it again and again – it will never be totally convincing.

You must practice with these weapons. Say them out loud in front of a mirror, with a colleague or your partner or both, regularly, consistently and like you mean it. The elite are the elite for one simple reason: they train hard so they can fight easy and therefore win time and again.

Efficient accounting time

This weapon is inspired by the work of Pareto, that clever Italian guy we talked about in chapter two. In this case, the 'efficient accounting tTime, or EAT, weapon is essentially a time-management conversation. It's used to sow larger, deeper seeds in your clients' minds. It is used at the rapport stage of the meeting and will reinforce the reputation for efficiency and professionalism that you've already been carefully building up ever since you first approached your prospect (and possibly even before, if they are a successful referral from another happy client). The EAT weapon is an effective way of explaining your situation and how you strive to run an efficient and effective diary that is to the total benefit of your valued client base.

How does it work?

Well, you begin by mentioning how much you admire and respect efficiency. The next step is to seamlessly switch to asking the prospect how they usually go about expanding their business and/or customer base. (Note the word 'seamlessly' here. This is why practice is essential. You don't want your client to be left wondering why you are leaping apparently randomly from one subject to another.) If you've pitched it right, the client will be happy to share their views. Let them explain to you how their company gains new contracts and supports this activity.

Once they have had their full say, it is your chance to deliver your killer blow. However, the customer won't consciously know it is your killer blow, because you will be using an oh-so-subtle 'drop it into conversation' technique. In this technique, what you say next is presented totally casually, as though the way you are behaving is the most natural way in the world to conduct yourself. (As, of course, it is.)

For this role-play, the prospect will be called Helen.

> **You:** 'Helen, I like to strive for efficiency in the way that I work. It is for this reason I've made a very

important promise to all the clients I have taken on before you. Today, I am going to make you the very same promise. But, let me explain a little background first, before I make it.

'I want to spend the majority of my time providing an excellent, thorough, well-considered service to my client base. This way, I find my personal client base grows naturally and very little of my time is spent, well, having meetings like this one when I am effectively trying to gain new clients. That should be taking up the minority of my energies.

'The only way I'm able to stick with this is to strive for everyone I meet to feel they have had a great consultation. Then, if they feel I am a credible guy and gave them an informed service where they benefit significantly, then they help me get to know a few people they know who would benefit from the same consultation.

'If I do this and my clients work with me, I find I spend far less time looking for new clients and am consequently able to give you, as my client, my all.

'I don't want you to worry about this right now and, of course, this only works if you benefit from what we are doing here today. I just wanted to flag up the parameters of professionalism that I like to work within and the types of relationship I like to forge. It's my own personal little rule, but it works pretty well for my clients and me.'

281 WORDS, 1 MINUTE 22 SECONDS (SHOT FIRED, TARGET HIT)

This 'drop it into the conversation' technique, when delivered well, works like a dream. Practice it thoroughly beforehand and then regularly after that, so you can deliver all the elements seamlessly. That way it won't become a sticking point that stops a previously promising meeting in its tracks. Just keep it light and casual, as though it is the most reasonable way of doing business in the world. Make your point well and move on. It will have the desired effect, I guarantee it.

If you're pushed for time, or prefer it short and sweet, there is a quick-fire, light-and-fast version.

Following the part when you asked them how their company gets new business, get in a 'yeah, similar to me' statement and say:

> **You:** 'I try to work as efficiently as possible, and generally this means working with my clients to assist me to meet more clients.
>
> 'It's just the most professional and effective use of my time.'

34 WORDS, 13 SECONDS (BOOM!)

> People come to you with a problem, whether it's buying a car, or sorting out their life insurance or their kids' education. If you do a good, thorough job, they'll go,

'Thank you, Chris, why don't you speak to my friends?'

If not, I use the old 80–20 rule and I say, 'Look, we've already spent three hours together in this week alone. Would you rather I spent my time looking after clients like you and giving you the service you need, or that I was distracted by going out and actively looking for new clients?'

They always say, 'With me.'

And I say, 'Great, well I do need your help, yeah? Who do you know that I don't who you think would benefit from the same level of professionalism you've had today?'

That works.

Chris Withers, Area Manager

Objective and subjective

This next weapon, which is also used at the opening stage of the meeting, is an absolute winner because it not only clarifies the whole process but also reinforces the exceptional value your client is about to gain from their consultation with you. If you don't use it for gaining referrals, just use it as a backbone for setting an agenda and managing expectations because, when used effectively, it instantly buys an enormous amount of professional credibility and trust.

The skill in making it work is to be totally sure of what you are going to say and how you are going to say it (yes, team, I am going to mention how important practice is, once again). Why? Because its success relies on how well you can employ your own words and intonation.

The passage of words you are about to use, or your own version of them, will synchronise easily with typical left-brain activity (if you don't remember what this is about, please refer back to chapter six). Essentially, though, it is pretty likely that, at this early stage in the meeting, the prospect is going to be in a left-brain-dominant thought pattern. Even if they are not naturally that way inclined, they will be gearing themselves up to process what you tell them analytically. After all, they are meeting a financial adviser, not a creative director for an art project. It doesn't matter whether they are usually right-brained thinkers – believe me, at this time, nine out of ten people will be deferring to the left hemisphere of their brain.

The beauty of this weapon is that it will help relax the prospect so they are more open to fully appreciating your objective, dogged approach to their finances.

This technique begins when you introduce the Fact Find questionnaire. Obviously you want the client to be familiar with this form. It helps them to fully understand what's about to take place and to respect and understand the true value of the process. It is also important to demonstrate to the client it is a genuine Fact Find, not some sort of trick designed to get them to do something they might not want to do. Your approach would go something like this.

> **You:** 'So, Helen, what we are going to do now is I am going to walk you through this financial questionnaire. This means I will need to ask you a series of questions about your financial life and, please, I need you to be as completely candid and accurate as possible.
>
> 'If you give me an accurate picture of your current situation, my advice will in turn be accurate. However, if you choose to distort it in any way, for whatever reason, then we will be wasting each other's time because you will end up with distorted advice too.'
>
> **Helen:** 'Okay, I understand that.'
>
> **You:** 'Great. So, as I progress through this questionnaire, we will probably identify a number of weak spots in your planning. These are areas you could use my help with.
>
> 'Now, I like to be quite direct when it comes to my observations, so can I just ask, is it OK if I am straight to the point when I see something you are doing that I, as a professional, think you shouldn't? Or should I soften things up a little? I just want to know the way to conduct this meeting in a manner that is most comfortable for you.'
>
> **Helen:** 'No, please be direct.' *(You'll get this response ninety-nine times out of a hundred.)*

221

You: 'That's great. We'll get on well. If I spot a problem that really needs to be looked at, I will point it out to you. If you agree you need advice on that aspect of your finances, I will simply flag it up with a little star and move on. If, however, you don't agree with me that something is a problem at all, despite my flagging it up, we will simply move past it. It is, after all, your money. However, I will know I've given you my best advice.

'At the end of the process, I fully expect there to be two or three areas that have been flagged up where we have both agreed you need help. If this is the case, I will ask you to instruct me to give you financial advice and we will move on to the next stage.'

Helen: 'Okay.'

You: 'Great. Okay, Helen, the way I look at the consultation I am about to give you is it divides into two very separate stages. There is the first phase, which is "objective," and then this is followed by the "subjective" phase. The first phase is, as I have already described, very much about me taking down facts and then using simple maths to identify and demonstrate areas of weakness to you from a purely professional viewpoint. The nature of this planning process is objective because it is purely factual and black and white. It's why I love this job. In maths everything is black and white. It either adds up or it quite simply doesn't.

'The second part of the process, the subjective one,

is where I recommend a solution, or set of solutions, to cure the problems we've uncovered in phase one. You may not like my prescriptions, or might even wish to seek a second opinion. It is totally up to you. I have no control over your free will and nor do I want any. My recommendations are born from my professional opinion. You may prefer the solution of the bank down the road, but I guarantee I will be providing you the very best consultation I can right now and will stand fully behind the value of everything I tell you. That is my focus for today.

'What I can also tell you is that you will, without a doubt, learn and gain benefit from this consultation, in which we will be creating a blueprint of your current financial situation and mapping out a route for the future.

'For that service I would like you to make me a small agreement. Before I even tell you what that agreement is, I will emphasise once again this is only relevant if this process is of benefit to you. If, however, you do see the benefit, the agreement I'd like you to make is that before I leave today we think of about five people you know who would also benefit from an exercise like this. In other words, if I impress you sufficiently, you would be happy to recommend me to others.

'Don't worry too much about it right now. We can brainstorm together at the end to come up with these names and find the most comfortable way for me to introduce myself to them. Right now, I just need to know you are in agreement with me and open to this process.'

Pause and wait for a nod of agreement. Acknowledge it and move straight into the Fact Find.

761 WORDS, 4 MINUTES 43 SECONDS (MAKE IT RAIN, BABY!)

In the dialogue above there are so many strong, positive selling phrases that your prospect will be putty in your hands. There are other ways this conversation can go, so it is well worth practising various scenarios so you can keep your prospect's attention and deliver them seamlessly to the door of referrals.[20]

Or there is the quick-fire, light-and-fast version:

You: 'Okay Helen, this is how the process works. Basically there are two phases to the process: objective and subjective. Objective is the part where I ask you what I call the "hard facts" and do the maths. From this exercise an accurate picture is framed and I provide you with a personal business plan for your life. Subjective is the part where I suggest a solution to any gaps we uncover in part one.

'The first part is my focus.

'The first part will be of huge benefit.

'The first part is what I'm sure your friends and colleagues will also love.'

---

20   For more examples, go to www.sales-commando.com.

103 WORDS, 42 SECONDS (BOOM, DOUBLE BOOM!)

Fact Find delivery

This final technique is a simple, yet powerful, strategy. It is best used once you've been through 'objective and subjective' thoroughly. It can be an integral part of the above approach; however, I have separated it out into a different section because it can be used independently too. Personally, I'd opt to use both techniques in conjunction with each other, because the more times you infer referrals the more success you will have with gaining them.

The choice is, of course, yours.

At the end of the objective–subjective speech, or whenever you judge to be the right moment if you are not following that technique, hold up the Fact Find and turn to the part where referrals are usually noted down. If you are someone who records referrals in a separate book, then this is the time to bring out that book.

> **You:** 'So, at the end of the meeting, we will be filling out this part here.'

Point to the section to get them visually familiar with it and get their acknowledgement. This technique is particularly powerful because, just as the old saying goes, seeing is believing. There can be no confusion over exactly what is meant by providing introductions, because it will be right there in black and white in front of the prospect. At a glance they'll be able to fully understand what is expected of them. To hit the jackpot, get the prospect to physically handle the book, or even read out loud the copy on the page. Emphasise what you are trying to do in what you say next.

> **You:** 'Okay, so when I say to think of people who would benefit from this process, what I mean is we will try to fill out this part here at the end of the meeting. See it there?'

You've got a real result if they read out loud the words on the referral page or the title of your referrals journal.

> **You:** 'I only want to talk to people you think I will get on with. I will help you brainstorm the right people if and when you agree you've benefited from this process.
>
> 'Plus, I absolutely want you to speak to these people first, before I contact them. In the unlikely event that they say to you, "Under no circumstances let that man call me," then I won't call them up, I assure you. I have no desire whatsoever to talk to people who don't want to talk to me. I just want you to know how and when this works, OK?'

153 WORDS, 49 SECONDS (OBSERVATIONS MADE, AGREED AND VERIFIED!)

Or, the quick-fire, light-and-fast version.

> **You:** 'Helen, just so you know, at the end of this process we are going to try to fill this out, just with people who will benefit from the service. There is no drama and let's try to get a few people you know who will like me. We can brainstorm who it will suit, OK?'

55 WORDS, 21 SECONDS (NO ONE IS MESSING

WITH YOU, YOU SPEED FREAK!)

At this point, depending on how you are getting on with the client, you can really bolt this technique to the ground using two further sub-techniques.

The first is to tell a third-party story.

> **You:** 'Please don't do to me what a guy last week did. He was agree, agree, agree, after I'd carried out a brilliant consultation that he was over the moon about. Then, when push came to shove, at the end of the meeting he then just totally changed his tune and said "no".'

The second sub-technique is brainstorming. Explain to the prospect that, when the time comes, you will help them brainstorm some names. This is extremely important because, as you will discover, once you do your magic, the clients' mind should be pretty fried, because it is so full of new concepts, facts and newly highlighted drivers. When they say they really can't think of anyone, they probably mean it. They really will be telling the truth. Assure them from the outset you'll always be there to help them picture things and think clearly.

> **You:** 'Now, when we get to the end of the meeting and if you're happy, I want to help you brainstorm the right type of person. I've got loads of ideas on how to do that.
>
> 'Remember, though, I just want to get their names down. I don't mean, 'Go away, think about it and email

me some ideas later.' Over the years I have waited for many emails to arrive and more often than not they don't. That's understandable, because we've all got busy lives to get on with and this won't be that important to you. However, it is clearly very important to me, so let's work together to get it done and out the way.'

Each of the weapons here is extremely powerful and has been tried and tested in action. Using just one will transform the way you go about referrals. Get to know and use them all and the sky really is the limit. However, as I have emphasised throughout this chapter, these weapons can only ever be as good as the person who handles them. It is up to you to get to know them, imagine and practice any little nuance and then do it again.

There are so many different ways to ask for referrals it's impossible to say I use one method. I do have personal preferences, but sometimes it depends on your mood, or more importantly the person you're with. As a consultant, one of the first skills you've got to have is to be able to judge people.

What I like to do is to understand that person to get a sense as to where I need to go with referrals and then go down that route. So, with some, if they are a very happy, jolly, funny, laughing person, you go down a certain route. If he's a serious person, you go a different route. You've just got to play it accordingly.

My preference is to leverage on the help. What I say is, 'Look, I'm going to help you today and you're going to see how much benefit you're going to get from that. Equally, I'm going to ask you to help me. You know people I don't know and, unless you don't like them, I presume you want me to help them as well.'

Noel O'Leary, Executive Director

Not only must the message be correctly delivered, but the messenger himself must be such as to recommend it to acceptance.[21]

---

21   J.B. Lightfoot, English theologian and Bishop of Durham (1828–1889).

Chapter nine

CLOSING EFFECTIVELY

Those who don't know how to get people to say yes fall away; those who do, stay and flourish.[22]

---

22   Robert B. Cialdini, Professor Emeritus of Psychology, Arizona State University (1945–).

I was quite insistent now and said, 'You want to pay by credit card or standing order?' He was still stalling though and saying he would do it later. When we got to the end of the paperwork, I said again, 'Are you going to pay by credit card or standing order?' He's like, 'Well...' So I said, 'Look, credit card is a pain in the ass. Standing order is much easier.'

This time, he replied, 'Yeah, right OK,' but still didn't make a move to give me the bank details. I could tell he was just waiting for me to go. Then he pipes up, 'Can we do that bit by email?'

I had to go back through all the reasons why we'd agreed the course of action in the first place. I had to be pretty persuasive, because it was clear he didn't want to commit, even then, but in the end he gave me all the details.'

Andrew Lockyer, Senior Consultant

Picture the scene. Out on a survival training exercise, two marines are being chased by the enemy. One of the pair is a corporal while the other's rank is marine. After a lengthy pursuit, they reach a deep ravine. The ravine is straddled by a rickety bridge held together with old rope that stretches across the sixty-foot gap. Looking down into the depths, the corporal estimates the deepest part of the ravine could be as much as a 200ft sheer drop, and there are razor-sharp rocks all the way.

The more junior marine hesitates at the crossing

because he is concerned about the strength and structure of the rope. He's really not at all convinced it will take their weight. He wonders out loud whether they'd be better off looking further up stream for a safer place to cross. The corporal says instantly, without hesitation, 'This rope can take our weight, plus anther troop of marines at the same time, easily! Now follow me.'

Off he goes, stepping confidently onto the bridge without a moment's delay.

The marine, hearing the confidence-building words and seeing the corporal's actions, instantly follows with comfort. They both cross successfully.

There is a great lesson here for us all.

The corporal knew he needed to instil confidence in the wavering marine, who clearly needed the comfort of belief at that second as he hesitated at the crossing. Even though the more senior marine privately shared the same worry, he was not going to let the man he led see this. Everything the corporal did, from the words he used to the way he deported himself, screamed: 'I am a confident person.'

If you want to lead and be the best at anything, this is how you must act: confidently, decisively and without fear. This is absolutely the case if you want to be a sales commando. When we sell, we lead.

I tell the above story at this point in the book because this, my friends, is what closing is all about: pure, simple and to a tee. Right now we are at the moment when you are going to make your final, powerful move that will blow your prospect's mind and will have them reaching for their very best signing pen.

Sure, there is a large number of things you need to do to build the sale beforehand and these things have all been carefully covered in the proceeding chapters. You'll have set up the meeting, talked your prospects through everything you know about your specialty (which is a lot), battled with a few fledgling objection monsters and secured a fistful of great referrals. But now, right at the end of the initial meeting – or at the second or third, which is often the 'time to sign the papers' meeting – is the moment when 99 per cent of prospects will suddenly have a last-minute wobble, or a concern to be addressed. It doesn't matter how well you've done up until now, the odds dictate they will have a moment of doubt.

Why? Well, even after all the positive reasons you have shown them as to why they *should* be doing something, most halfway intelligent people will actively seek out all of the reasons why they *shouldn't*. You can't blame them for this – we all do it. So, don't waste any time worrying about the fact they're having a wobble; concern yourself with how you are going to lead them out of it.

This, over and above all other times, is the moment you must lead, and lead with strength. Your mission is to close the deal decisively. This means you must have an answer for absolutely any last-minute objection your prospect flings at you. That answer must roll past your lips automatically, without hesitation, and be said with complete, unshakeable conviction. If you have to think about what you are saying at these moments, or have to pause to remember what you'd always planned to say, or if you stumble, or jitter, or waffle through your pre-prepared script, then you lose. You don't close. The marine does not follow you and the whole shooting match was a complete waste of time.

So, team, let's learn to close like a pro.

Closing master class

The first, most vital lesson in closing is to understand a close is *always* required and must *always* be used.

It doesn't matter if you've constructed your meeting in the most perfect manner ever. I don't care if your prospect has been nodding away in agreement all the way through like a demented teenage headbanger at a rock concert. It doesn't even matter if they have revealed every personal detail you've asked for and a few more besides. Similarly, if they've already reeled off a few potential referrals, that doesn't mean it is time to relax and begin mentally totting up your commission.

Sure, closing will be easier if they've already shown they're keen, but that doesn't mean you can let your guard down. You still have to follow the closing process – although, granted, the effort and persistency you need to achieve the close should be less arduous.

The second important lesson in this closing master class is to make sure you understand that closing is a *completely different* discipline from selling.

Closing is not selling. Closing is closing. You have already sold everything you've gone in to sell. All the prospect has to do now is just do it. Closing is the 'call to action'. It is:

» the transaction
» the irreversible agreement
» what you are there for
» the defining moment that will change the prospect's life for the better.

Yet, at this pivotal moment, far too many salespeople blow it. Why? Well, did you know the biggest single reason why customers don't actually buy a product is because they are *never actually asked to* by the person selling it to them?

In my capacity as a sales trainer, I've observed many, many financial consultants in meetings with potential clients. Very often they'll carry out amazing consultations, providing the client with fantastic advice and solutions to their financial issues, and, hardly surprisingly, gain maximum interest from the would-be client. Then, astonishingly, they don't ask for the business. Not even once. Inexplicably, they leave the meeting with a promise to send the client an email report or to book in a follow-up meeting without really stating the purpose for that subsequent meeting. They might say something vague about returning to sort out the paperwork, but that is about as far as it goes. It can hardly be a surprise to hear that a consultant who does this may never get a decision. The prime moment for closing was lost. This consultant sold brilliantly, but he didn't make a call to action. He will never, ever be in such a strong position with this prospect again.

Prospects almost never come right out and say, 'Great, I'd like to do this right now because I can see it will transform my future. Where do I sign?' It doesn't matter how interested they are. In fact, they'll probably be OK about letting the whole moment go if you don't come right out with it and ask them.

Look at it another way. If you are anything like me, you probably spend a great deal of time surfing the internet, either researching some product you have an interest in or following up on an advert you've seen. Once you've clicked on the website promoting product X, you think, 'Yeah, this is quite cool, I might get one of these,' and you look around for the 'buy' button. If, for whatever reason, you can't immediately find the buy button, or you do click on it and the purchasing process turns out to be so complicated you need a Ph.D. in nuclear physics to decipher it, you will give up immediately. With one click you'll be on your way.

The reason this website lost your interest – and, crucially, your business – is because the design of the site was not good enough to 'close you' and get the transaction done. It focused too much on selling and didn't give any, or at least enough, thought to closing. Yet, there you were, primed and ready to buy. You liked the product and intended to get it. After your experience, it is quite possible you'll make a mental note to go back to it again 'when you have more time', but you won't. Not ever. You'll be in the ranks of the coulda, shoulda but didn't for that product through no fault of your own. The call to action was not made and you were never closed properly.

So, if you are guilty of not making a call to action the definitive end to your meetings as a matter of routine, it is time to change. Make your closing strategy a priority because, if you don't, everything else you've learnt here will be a complete waste of time.

If it helps to strengthen your resolve, let me refresh you and focus your mind on some facts. My life won't change much if I don't buy some gadget I was looking at on the internet because I couldn't work out how to actually buy it. My future will probably be pretty much the same if I don't buy that leather coat that I tried on in the store because I was being served by some dopey teenager with a couldn't-be-bothered attitude who managed to get my size and hand me the jacket without actually saying a single word (a talent in itself). However, if I don't plan properly for my retirement, or make sufficient provision for my family, that will be a real problem.

Let's take it as a given that we are all providing sound

financial advice that is spot on for the client. If we make this assumption, it is an unquestionable fact that every single person who isn't closed, or whom we don't attempt to close, or whom we let off the hook at the first delay or objection, is being let down by their adviser in a very big way. By fluffing the close, you'll be allowing them to carry on with their dysfunctional financial lives in which they are doing nothing significant towards their retirement, are not protecting themselves or their loved ones and are generally throwing their hard-earned cash away. You'll have seriously let them down.

Shame on you. Have a word with yourself.

We financial advisers, more than any profession on planet Earth, need and must be able to close. It's our duty to close the deal. It's our mission to close the deal, to get the signature, to transact, to gain commitment, to create action and get decisions that will affect the prospect's life for the better.

As a final point (and this should go without saying after all we've been through in this book, but here goes), don't give up at the first rebuttal. If you try closing once and get knocked back, try again. Not attempting to get past an initial setback is not sales commando behaviour. Your mission is to get this sale closed. There are no excuses.

Observational note to be aware of here: the largest and most common 'excuse boat' that is launched by less ambitious salespeople generally sails upon one or more of the following:

» 'Ah, but I don't want to come across too pushy'
» 'I will lose the deal'
» 'They will feel pressurised and that's not good'
» 'I can't do that – it will sour the deal.'

There is enough hot air behind each of these excuse boats to help them sail far, far away, taking with them all of these misguided thoughts and your new potential deal too. *Burn these boat now.*

You shouldn't need reasons to follow this advice, but here are two: firstly, when you conduct yourself professionally and confidently, your client will never think like that. Secondly, I guarantee you that the line of offence – namely, the line you are afraid of crossing lest you offend the prospect – is far deeper into their territory than you could ever imagine. *Fear* – or what we might think of as a 'false event appearing real' – is popping its head up.

If you still require some comfort and confidence to march into these new, deeper territories, try a couple of the following techniques. These simple responses will pacify the would-be offended, or pressurised, prospect in the *extremely unlikely* event that this ever does actually become reality.

> **Prospect:** 'I don't like to be pressurised/squeezed/forced/rushed.'
>
> **You:** 'Please don't mistake my passion for doing the right thing by you as pressure. I am saying this because I know you need to do this and I believe you do also.'

32 WORDS, 13 SECONDS

> **You:** 'Hey, please don't misread my passion and professionalism and interpret it as pressure. I can't help getting passionate when I see an obvious need to act, because I believe in what I do so much.'

35 WORDS, 16 SECONDS

> **You:** 'I'm sorry, I can see you're getting uncomfortable. Please don't misinterpret my passion for doing the right thing, or mistake my professionalism for pressure.'

24 WORDS, 12 SECONDS

> **You:** 'I can see you're getting a little bothered by my persistence and passion to get this done and, you know what, I'm glad, because it's something you absolutely should do and it at least means I am trying hard enough. Please don't confuse my passion with pressure.'

47 WORDS, 19 SECONDS (SITUATION SORTED, DEAL PROTECTED!)

I personally first observed this way of dealing with this type of negotiation scenario when selling hot tubs at the London Ideal Home Show back in the year 2000. I learnt it from two Canadian salespeople I flew over to the UK to help me and my team with sales at the show, and it worked like a dream. I have been using it and teaching it for years. Again, let's face it, convincing someone to do something positive about their finances is something you truly can and should get passionate about. These techniques hardly ever need to be used, but, if they do, they will provide you with the necessary confidence to press harder for your objective, and using them will make any ill feeling disappear.

> I do something I call 'dragging up the objections' because, as I always say, an objection should be welcomed, not feared. When a client has a last-minute hesitation, I say, 'Right, I've explained everything I can to the best of my abilities. We've gone through all the plans on the market but, now we've gone for X, there seems to be some cause for hesitation about going ahead right now. May I ask what it is? Is it the money?'
>
> The client might reply, 'No, it's not the money.'
>
> So, I go through the list of possible objections and ask, 'What else is there?'
>
> If you actually go down that process and say, 'What else? What else? What else?' you will generally find the last one they give you is the true objection. Once I've got to the bottom of it, I say, 'What would it take to satisfy you on that question?'
>
> If you answer that objection, you've got them as a client.
>
> ***Chris Withers, Area Manager***

Be outcome orientated

To close effectively, you need to communicate your desired outcome for the meeting as early in the process as you can, and certainly at some stage in the rapport-building stage, while the client is relaxed. This is the way to ensure maximum impact and results.

Let's not mince our words, though. You need to be confident enough to say exactly why you are there. (Remember our corporal from the chapter opening? Confidence is key.) So, what is your true desire? What is the precise reason you are meeting this person? Simple: you want their business. You want to take them on as a client. That's it. In a nutshell. So tell them that. Communicate this from the off, particularly if they show you an early driver; that way, it will be a lot easier to reignite that driver at the close.

Some examples of 'drop it in'-type sentences you might use include:

» 'Great to meet you today. Hey, let me be clear, the ultimate reason I'm here is to formally take you on as a client and to do business with you to some degree. Obviously there are a number of hoops we'll need to go through today and you need to be happy about everything, but I always want to be upfront and let people know what I'd like to happen. So, tell me a little more about yourself.'
78 WORDS, 28 SECONDS (THE MAN IS BRIEFED)

» 'Hey, I'm here because I want to help you and continue helping you financially. That's why I've met you.'

19 WORDS, 7 SECONDS (WHACK!)

» 'I want you to view the way we will be working together going forwards very much on a relationship footing, a professional one, but a relationship none the less. I like to get to know all my clients so I can be in tune with their financial goals and ensure I help them to achieve them. I'm here today because I'd like to take you on as a client. So, tell me a little more about what makes you tick financially.'

81 WORDS, 27 SECONDS (YOU ARE A SALES HERO)

Get any one of these comments in straight away, or use them all. Say them before any barriers have gone up and make it sound as if each one is an absolutely obvious, no-brainer type of statement. Because it is.

Early airing of the idea of an imminent call to action makes a huge difference. It is very similar to the referrals strategy, where it's good to mention it as soon as possible, while the client is relaxed and certainly before they go into 'business brain' mode. After you've introduced it, it is a lot easier to continually drop in references throughout the meeting.

Just remember: let them know, let them know early, let them know often. This means that, by the actual close, you will be able to simply go for the transaction. The aim is to close well, close firmly and close persistently. Persistence and consistency are the keys to successful selling – indeed, more so in the close than in any other aspect of the process.

Closing weapons

To help you in this final stage of your sale, I have once again placed a range of powerful weapons at your disposal. Just as in the referral weapons section, it is up to you to work out which ones suit you best. However, as before, my advice is to perfect them all, because different set-piece plays may be more appropriate in different circumstances.

Again, please do feel free to place your own words into the format. Most importantly, pre-rehearse and practice these techniques on a daily basis. Deliver them with utter passion and conviction and you will close more deals.

The closing circle

The closing circle (Fig 3) is a simple technique to help you visualise the close and be methodical when doing it. The idea is to refresh the prospect's mind with all the things that were important to them in the process of summarising the key points of the products you've

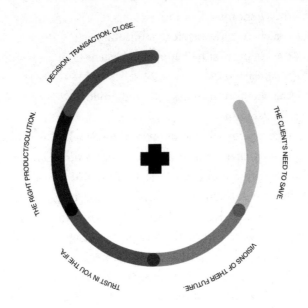

Fig 3

been discussing. This means covering each aspect of the financial advice you've mentioned as well as the product or solution you have designed to fit their laid-down criteria. Running through the main points of the discussion will naturally lead to the 'no-brainier' decision to commit to the transaction. You simply state this is the case and get the client's firm agreement and signature.

The closing circle is used to bridge the sale to the close and then keep your prospect in the close until the

transaction is finalised. The key areas to consider are:
 » the client must be motived
 » the client must be clear about the need
 » the client must be happy with you as their financial adviser
 » the client must understand the product
 » the decision.

Once you get to the point in the *sale* when you are happy the client is *sold enough*, bridge from selling to closing with a round-up of each of the first four points above, seeking affirmations on each one to create the bridge to the decision. Simply keep rotating around those categories until the prospect is happy and says 'yes'. Then you've got a decision. Simple!

Depending on the way you and your organisation work, there may or may not be legally binding documentation available to be signed there and then. If there isn't, you should still ensure you seek the client's agreement and commitment, whether via a simple handshake or a signature on a hand-written heads of agreement or both.

Don't forget, you want this transaction. You want to close and you want commitment in as many forms as possible until you next meet with the actual documents.

The closing circle is a great tool to help you do this. It can also be used to persist with the close, even after the first objection, the second and the third.

Let me map out a little potential role-play here.

> **You:** 'So, we are happy this is what we need to do?'

(Accompany statement with positive body language, such as nodding and smiling.)

Client: 'Yes.'

You: 'The reasons for it are clear. It's going to fully address the issue and the product and provider are first class, agreed?'

Client: 'Yeah.'

33 WORDS, 14 SECONDS

Then, follow one of the two following paths, depending on your working practices. If you are able to sign papers right then:

You: 'Great, so that's that then. Please sign here and here. By the way, your policy details will be with you in about two weeks, so welcome on board.'

28 WORDS, 11 SECONDS

Or, if you are in a meeting in which official paperwork is yet to be drawn up:

You: 'Great, so that's that then. Glad you're on board. I'm going to really enjoy working with you. Just to re-affirm, I will be back here on [state date and time] and I will bring with me all the necessary paperwork, all pre-populated as much as I can. There will be big "sign here" stickers on all the places you are required to make a signature.

'For now, just let me list all the things this covers and a heads of agreement.'

81 WORDS, 27 SECONDS

Then, taking a yellow legal notepad – which you can

very cheaply acquire from any good stationer – write out all the key factors: what the prospect is doing, why they are doing it and the product's key facts. Place big ticks next to all the reasons the client wanted, or needed, to do each action in the first place. For example:

» massive pension shortfall (tick)

» need to retire at a certain age (tick)

» want further control of investment strategy (tick).

Sign the agreement yourself and then turn the book around to get the client to sign it too. Re-affirm the date and time of the next meeting to sign paperwork, rapport them down and exit the meeting.

Remember: be clear, calm and confident – the big three Cs – at all times.

Delays or rebuttals using the closing circle

If you get an objection or a delaying rebuttal in the closing stages, as you attempt to transact, tackle it in the following way.

> **You:** 'So, you are happy this is what you need?'
>
> **Client:** 'Well, no, not really.'
>
> **You:** 'Oh, please tell me why.' (*Flush out the sticking point and deal with it using techniques learnt from the objections section. Then get back into the closing loop.*)
>
> Alternatively, if you get a vague answer like this:
>
> **Client:** 'I just need time to think about it…'
>
> Tackle it like this:
>
> **You:** 'Hey, I agree. However, thought is an instant

thing. Look, we agreed on the reasons why you need and want to do this, right?'

Client: 'Yeah.'

You: 'You know and understand that you need a product like this, right?'

Client: 'Hmm, yeah.'

You: 'You are happy with me as an adviser?'

Client: 'Yes.'

You: 'You know this addresses the problems, right?'

Client: 'Yes.'

You: 'There, we've thought about it. Let's take action then and get this done.'

Now, close them.

If you get a further delaying tactic along the following lines:

Client: 'But I just want more time to decide…'

Tackle it like this:

You: 'As I have said, I totally understand. Let me help you with that. Let's take a look at each part in detail again.'

Go into each point of the closing circle until you come back around to the 'let's take action now' part.

Stick with the closing circle for a *minimum* of two passes. If you have pre-prepared four different re-approaches, it will encourage you to try different tactics at least a few times. This in itself will improve your closing ratio enormously and will certainly give you much greater chances of success than if you just stick to one standard rebuttal every time. In fact, you'll be amazed at how much of a closing machine this will make you. Work hard and do it right and I guarantee you will rocket to the top percentages of the highest-performing financial advisers.

Pros and cons list (the good old Ben Franklin close)
This is simple and effective. Just because it's hundreds of years old does not mean it's not as good today as it ever was. I have used this technique so many times, possibly running into the thousands over the years, and it has worked with pretty much everything I've ever sold in my life. It's also frequently been used on me and I don't mind one bit. In fact, I actually get lots out of the process when I am encouraged to make a decision. I even use the technique on myself to help me work things though when I've got choices to make.

It works well because, when you close, you need to be methodical, calm and logical. You also need to be thorough and visual. I would personally use this technique on the first rebuttal, but you can also use it on the initial round-up and summary.

Begin by listing all the reasons the prospect needs to save, or invest, or insure, or do whatever it is they need to do to sort out their financial lives. Then, list all the reasons against. These are the pros. Without fail, the pros will always outweigh the cons.

The trick here is to get the prospect to come up with all the cons and it's vital you get them to voice them out loud, too. If needs be you can openly help them brainstorm the reasons they should not do what is clearly best for them. It won't take long.

Similarly, you then need to coach, suggest and work with the prospect to create a list of reasons why they should actually take the course of action you've suggested. If you've given the right advice, this list will always be infinitely larger and the individual reasons will also be noticeably more compelling.

The strength of this approach is you are both objectively working together and allowing the facts to speak for themselves. There is still a need to close the meeting off and bolt it down; however, you will be amazed at the power of this pros and cons approach.

The contrast between the positive and negative points on the list should crack even the toughest of nuts, assuming you have done a reasonable job in the rest of the sales process, of course.

Slipping the sign-up: Set-piece plays

To finish this chapter, I have scripted several set-piece plays for most common objections or rebuttals at closing time. As with all the set-piece plays throughout this book, they work best if you rehearse and memorise them. Practice them daily and you will close more deals.

These scenarios may occur over the phone or face to face.

Insistence close 1

Client: 'I want to leave it six months.'

You: 'Okay, but may I ask what the reasons were that you came to see me in the first place? Basically, if I read this right, up until now every professional you have sat before has accepted your reasons for avoiding what you know you should do. I'm afraid I'm not going to let my professional standards slip and let you down by allowing that to happen again. I'm coming to see you tomorrow with everything totally prepared. All I need is a few signatures and you have crossed a big job of your *must* do list. How about 10am, or 2pm, or shall we say 6pm?'

106 WORDS, 35 SECONDS (BULLET DODGED, FIRE RETURNED)

Insistence close 2

Client: 'I want to wait a while; it's a bad time.'

You: 'I know what it's like. There is always going to be something else to pay for, or something else you want to buy, or some other thing pressing for the allocation of your money. These demands are all immediate and that's why they gain your attention. What we are doing here and now is about your tomorrow and, even though it's very easy to tell yourself tomorrow never comes, it does. You and I both know you need to do this right now. Time is upon us. So, I'm going to come and see you tomorrow with everything ready. I just need some signatures and then I'll be on my way. You can then tick a very large box on your *must* do list. Midday, 4pm, or 6-ish?'

128 WORDS, 50 SECONDS

Insistence close 3

Client: 'I'm not ready to start this.'

You: 'Ha, yeah, no one is ever ready to put money away for their future selves. It's just not rock and roll, is it? However, like it or not, it is essential, so please listen to me. I'm not going to let you down by accepting your excuse. I'm going to come and see you tomorrow with everything prepared. All I will need is a few signatures and you will have done a huge job that you've been putting off forever. Now, 10am or 2pm?'

84 WORDS, 29 SECONDS

Insistence close 4

Client: 'I need to think about it for longer.'

You: 'I hear what you are saying; however, that is not a reason to delay. Thought is instantaneous and the truth is that you are finding an excuse to put off things you know you should do. I'm not going to let you do that. I'm too professional and you're too important to me for me to let that happen. I'm coming to see you tomorrow with absolutely everything prepared. I just require some signatures from you and you can relax knowing you have done something positive for your future self. How about 10am, or 2pm or 4pm?'

97 WORDS, 32 SECONDS

Honest investigation close 1

Client: 'Hmmm, I'll contact you when I'm ready.'

You: 'Lots of people say this. However, very few do ever come back at a later date. I know that the real reason they say it is that they are polite people who are just putting something off because they are not totally convinced. So come on, level with me, what is it you are not totally convinced about?'

58 WORDS, 22 SECONDS

(This set-piece play will open the way to gaining a clearer picture of the objection. Deal with the objection according to the three-phase process detailed in chapter five, then insist and close.)

Honest investigation close 2

Client: 'Let me cover it off with my wife.'

You: 'Yeah, people say this to me from time to time. May I be honest with you?'

Client: 'Yes.'

You: 'It's an excuse. You make decisions all the time and this is a firm positive decision she will thank you for making. It's better to ask for forgiveness than permission in situation like this. So come on, I need your signature here and here.'

60 WORDS, 22 SECONDS

Feel, felt, found close

Client: 'I'm not sure it feels right.'

You: 'Hey, many people feel the exact same way as

you, so it's pretty normal to say and indeed think that. However, what these people also find is, once they have signed the paperwork, they always feel an enormous sense of relief for doing something positive for their future selves. So, let's do something positive today and not negative. I need your signature here and here.'

65 WORDS, 28 SECONDS

Soft close

Client: 'I'm still not 100 per cent…'

You: 'Okay, so what I'm going to do is leave you with these product details and then, by this afternoon, I will have pre-populated all the documents you need to sign and will email them to you. Please print them out and just sign them where I have indicated. I will then collect them and forwards them to the institution to apply to get your account open. I'll drop in tomorrow to collect the paperwork. Is morning, afternoon or evening good for you?'

82 WORDS, 29 SECONDS

Lump-sum soft close

Client: 'I'm still not 100 per cent…'

You: 'Okay, so we understand that we need to get this money working for you, yes? What I'm going to do is set up the account that the cash is going to travel into and get everything ready for you. I simply need a few signatures, then we just have to shift the money across. It is effectively taking it from one pocket and then putting it into another one where it has the best and steadiest opportunity of gaining growth.'

80 WORDS, 25 SECONDS

The three-reasons close

Client: 'I want to think about things a little longer.'

You: 'I understand. Hey, it's got to be the right thing, right? If I may say there are, in my experience, only three reasons why someone says this: they don't fully understand how much they really need to be doing this; I have not conducted myself in a way that instils complete trust; or I have made an error in the way we have done your budgets and the amount you're saving is too high. Now, which one is it: one, two or three?'

83 WORDS, 36 SECONDS (THEY'RE ON THE RUN)

Last-attempt closes

You: 'Okay, what are the circumstances that need to be created for you to sign the documents now and get this sorted? Come on, let's create them.'

26 WORDS, 13 SECONDS

Or,

You: 'Okay, you know this needs to be done. You understand the way the product works. I always do things this way and my handshake is my bond.' *(Lean over to shake their hand and welcome them as a client.)*

27 WORDS, 10 SECONDS

Or,

> **You:** 'Hey, this situation will not get any easier. The more you put this off, the greater the issue becomes. I'm not going to allow this situation to get worse for you. I like you too much for that, so come on, take positive action now. Let's get this sorted.'

49 WORDS, 20 SECONDS

Train repetitively, so it becomes instinctive

Closing must be rehearsed again and again because you must go into the close with utter confidence, just like the marine corporal. Be calm and act like a true leader at this point and you will succeed. Simply accept every prospect will have some kind of fear working through in their mind, no matter how small, and resolve to deal with it. Lead the prospect though their doubts with a sturdy, methodical, factual and calculated approach. That is the way of a sales commando.

> If I get to the second, sign-up, meeting and the client suddenly wobbles, I always view it as my fault. Let's take it to the extreme and say the client says, 'Actually, I'm buying a house.' To me that's a euphemism for, 'You've got something wrong.' It means I've missed something.

The majority of people will not give you the honest reason as to why they don't want to buy from you at the last minute. They will prefer to give you a smokescreen.

An analogy I use to describe this behaviour is as follows. Say I'm in a television shop with my daughter. I know nothing about televisions, I really don't have a clue. If the guy from the shop starts talking to me about the inner mechanisms of the televisions, he'll be talking at a level I just don't get. I will look at him and say, 'Yeah, I've got to go and see my wife,' and I'll just leave. I won't be going to see my wife. I'll probably be doing something else completely, but it will be an excuse to leave the shop. If the TV salesperson has his wits about him, he'll look at me and see I'm with an eleven-year-old girl. He might say, 'This television has got 3D and it's great for kids' movies.' Then he's got me because he's actually looked to see what's relevant to me.

If you come up against an objection in the second meeting, it's a sign you haven't read the client's signal properly

or dealt with something appropriately in
the first meeting.

Noel O'Leary, Executive Director

*Sometimes we stare so long at a door that is closing that we see
too late the one that is open.*[23]

---

23   Alexander Graham Bell, scientist and inventor (1847–1922).

AFTERWORD

This, team, is the moment of truth. In this book I have given you all the weapons you need to go out there and become the best sales professionals you can possibly be. In each chapter, there are nuggets of gold, exercises, tips and examples that will equip you with the skills you need to either begin, enhance or polish your selling techniques and professionalism and set you on the road to becoming a master of your industry.

It is my firm hope that just reading what I've got to say, together with the words of those established sales professionals who kindly helped in this endeavour, will be enough to put you into the mindset of a successful sales professional. Everything here works and has been proven to do so again and again. All you need to do to make it to the top of today's competitive marketplace is pick these techniques up, run with them and make them your own. Any one of the ideas set out here will help you achieve the very best results every day, over and over again. Use them all and you will become a very powerful force indeed. As if that isn't enough, this book offers you all the ammunition you need to ensure you build a network of people who will become your allies out there in the marketplace. Get it right and they'll be singing your praises to anyone and everyone so you will never, ever be short of quality people to meet ever again.

Now it is time for the caveat, though. In my experience, anyone who wants to learn the art of selling can do so. Indeed, it's something we all do to a certain extent in our day-to-day lives anyhow, whether or not we follow it as a profession. However, the degree to which you are successful in sales as a career is very much down to you. The level of success you achieve, or otherwise, depends largely on how much you really want to be the best. Your chances of reaching the top 20 per cent, that higher level of super-salespeople, depends upon your level of commitment. I'm afraid it is just like what they used to tell you at school: your level of achievement correlates directly with the amount of effort you put in.

To put it more simply, it is all down to desire. Those who don't achieve the level of sales success they imagined usually didn't want it badly enough in the first place. If you don't have a burning passion to succeed, you almost certainly won't.

Take putting in the time behind the scenes, for example. Becoming the best in sales is something you have to fully buy into with a passion. One of the themes I have returned to again and again in this book is practice, because practice really does make perfect. Good selling isn't a case of getting in front of someone and talking your head off until they give in. They won't. You have to hone your technique beforehand, work out the answers to every possible question and go over them again and again so that, when you do say anything, it comes out as the most natural (and most convincing) response in the world.

If you aspire to be one of the sales elite, you need to learn how to tailor your pitch to the listener every time, and the only way you'll do that is if you practice over and over again. That way, you won't just be telling them what you *think* they care about, you'll be so on top of your subject you'll *know* what is important to them.

If your reaction to this is, 'I haven't got time,' or, 'I devote enough of my working day to sales, so I'm not going to do anything extra at home,' you will be permanently stuck in the slow lane. You don't want it badly enough. Stop reading this book because you're wasting my time. Sure, you might feel a bit of a berk standing in front of a mirror convincing your own reflection to consider this product or that, but it's this additional work, borne out of passion for the job, that will put you out in front. Knowing your pitch inside out, backwards and sideways – and all its associated possible variations, objections or potential rejections – will transform your sales career. Your goal should be to mentally perfect your portfolio of responses so that, when the client asks the perfectly reasonable question, 'Why should I do business with you?' you'll come straight back with a killer reply.

Your research should also extend to the person you're going to see. Who are they? What is their background? How can your products solve their problems? You may be promoting the best product in the world, but, if you can't get across how it will help that person, you'll be seen as a time waster.

If you are serious about becoming one of the sales elite, this is the level of commitment you need. Nothing else will do. I won't kid you. It's not easy and it will require an almost super-human effort. But that level of difficulty shows just how much it is worth having.

No one is going to smooth the way and make it easier for you. Nor should you expect them to. Indeed, if anything, the sales environment is getting tougher all the time. Modern salespeople are under fire from all directions. Thanks to the internet, the consumer is markedly more savvy and far more likely to question pretty much everything you say. In the worst-case scenario they may even have built up a strong wall of resistance to pretty much anything you tell them. Meanwhile, following the global economic collapse in 2008, we are all still faced with an environment of severe cost-cutting among both individuals and organisations. No one spends cash any more unless they are 100 per cent certain they are getting good value and, even then, they'll take some convincing. Added to this there is a constant tightening up and adjustment of the rules governing financial sales, which can make a tough job well-nigh impossible in some regions of the world.

Yet, for all the same reasons this job is getting tougher, there is more opportunity for the canny salesperson. Prove you know what you are talking about and display an unshakeable confidence and grasp of the fiscal environment, and half the job is already done. While other, lesser, salespeople are scrabbling about, apologising for their very presence, you can look your prospects square in the eyes in the sure knowledge you are doing them a real favour by agreeing to help them. How powerful is that?

If you truly believe in what you do, you will out-perform the waiverers and doubters every time. Your belief will be transmitted in everything you do and everything you say. Prospects will be blown away by your genuine conviction and enthusiasm.

This is what it takes to succeed as one of the sales elite. It will take time and effort to perfect your pitch, but the rewards will make it worth your while. Those who reach the top in this business can look forwards to a very lucrative living in a varied and fulfilling career that may well take them all over the world. It is worth your while.

Are you ready to become one of the sales elite? Good.

Take what you've learnt here, practice it, perfect it and earn your place as a sales commando. You won't regret it.

Doug Tucker

www.sales-commando.com

APPENDIX

Who's Who'

Graham Bentley, Senior Area Manager

Graham has more than 17 years of financial and sales experience and is a fully qualified International Advisor. His main area of expertise is personal wealth management and he has been awarded the Top Global Financial Advisor Award in four out of the last five years by the world's largest independent advisory company. He enjoys spending his spare time with his wife and three children and also regularly undertakes regular charity challenges for his company's foundation.

David Hughes, Divisional Manager

Having initially studied in business and finance, David started his career in retail and then moved into telecommunications, rising to director level before going back to finance. David is a keen believer of leading by example and has always set his own targets and then broken them. He loves being set a challenge which he invariably completes with a smile on his face.

Andrew Lockyer, Senior Consultant

Andrew left university in 2007 with a degree in

economics and started working as a coordinator for the deVere group in Qatar. In his first year for the company he became its top-ranking telephone coordinator worldwide and he moved to Dubai in 2009 to be a consultant within the same company. In 2013, he was named as one of the company's top ten consultants.

Noel O'Leary, Executive Director

After completing a Degree in Business and Law, Noel has spent the last 20 years in the banking and personal finance industry where he has received numerous awards both as a financial advisor and as a manager. He has gained a reputation for providing client-focused, holistic and independent advice to the highest of standards as well as developing numerous advisors to realise their full potential in the industry. After spending five years in Geneva, in 2013 Noel swapped the ski slopes of Switzerland for the desert of Dubai where he enjoys a life of sunshine in the sand with Martina and Hannah.

Andrew Oliver, Senior Area Manager

Andrew studied modern languages at Leeds University and was subsequently commissioned into the Army (Parachute Regiment) in 1989. He entered the financial services sector in 1995 and has striven to be at the top of his game. He is keen on personal fitness and likes to maintain a keen sense of humour by being a Sunderland fan.

Duncan Raeside, Senior Wealth Manager

Duncain was born and raised in Hertfordshire and graduated from the University of Newcastle Upon Tyne in 2001 with a BSc Hons degree in Computer Science. He began his career as a business analyst with PriceWaterhouseCoopers in London before moving to overseas in 2005. After a few years as a Business Development Manager in the IT industry, he retrained as an IFA.

Steve Rigby, Divisional Manger

Steve began his career in the Air Force in 1980, working in the administration branch. After training as an accountant he moved to the accounts division of the Air Force to manage the Armed Forces' pensions scheme. Following a tour of four years in Dhahran on a Special Duties assignment, Steve decided to stay in the Middle East and moved to the UAE. After investing with PIC in 1995 he began working with them in 1999 and has been in the UAE ever since along with his wife Rachael and children Rebekka and Sam. In his spare time he keeps fit and is an avid follower of all things sport, with golf, rugby and football being the favourites.

Chris Withers, Area Manager

Chris left Leeds University in 1998 and began his sales career as a car salesmen, which was essentially a summer job to pay off his student loan. He moved to

Singapore as a coordinator for a large international financial services company in 1998 and became the top coordinator there. He then moved to Dubai and studied to become a UK qualified financial advisor. He now manages a team and is achieving £400K + per year in personal issued business.